I0005892

3D Hardware design:

Software applications for GPU

S Mathioudakis

authorHOUSE®

AuthorHouse™ UK
1663 Liberty Drive
Bloomington, IN 47403 USA
www.authorhouse.co.uk
Phone: UK TFN: 0800 0148641 (Toll Free inside the UK)
UK Local: (02) 0369 56322 (+44 20 3695 6322 from outside the UK)

Published by AuthorHouse 12/10/2025

ISBN: 979-8-8230-9162-6 (sc)
ISBN: 979-8-8230-9163-3 (e)

Library of Congress Control Number: 2025900569

Print information available on the last page.

CONTENTS

FOREWORD

Working in three dimensions opens up more opportunities for producing software applications. The concept itself demands a number of techniques to assess mathematical assumptions and hardware choices. The text intends to offer the reader a chance to evaluate the subject from both a programming and hardware perspective. The text is aimed at programmers with an interest in designing hardware concepts and design.

PREFACE

This text looks at the topic of three-dimensional programming and some of the concepts and mathematics underpinning the subject. Due to the precedence of applications that can use this discipline, it is an important part of a computer's hardware and software design. The text highlights how three-dimensional programs are constructed and how they can function inside the computer's hardware. Throughout the text are diagrams and example code that describe how the procedures work and the mathematics that the subject is created from. The principle is that due to the many concepts that underpin languages such as OpenGL and GFWL there are several considerations when attempting to begin learning or writing programs within this type of code.

The text itself is written from a hardware perspective, as understanding how the computer is intended to function not only improves the code but allows the reader to develop their knowledge of computerized systems. For this reason, the text aims to look at the mathematics needed to create the programs and the ASM formatted code, which describes how the hardware functions during routines.

PART 1

Three-dimensional Principles and Mathematics

CHAPTER 1

The Graphics Pipeline

In this chapter, you will look at the following

- How graphics processors work
- The graphics pipeline
- Interpreting geometric shapes
- Rendering and shading an object

1.1.1 The importance of 3D processing?

Many modern computers rely on extensive code libraries that enable them to process information in three dimensions. For example, many games and software like AutoCAD allow users to create objects that can be resized, modified, and used in different environments. The advantages of these applications include the ability to visualize projects before the design phase and generate graphics that can simulate real-time physics. Today, modern computers are equipped with dedicated Graphics Processing Units (GPUs) that handle graphical processes. This technology allows computers to visualize geometric information and render objects effectively. Due to the wide range of applications, this topic has become crucial in the design of computerized systems.

USES OF GRAPHICAL PROCESSORS	
PHYSICS SIMULATIONS	Virtual worlds
ENGINEERING DESIGN	Geometry and excavation
ARCHITECTURE DESIGN	Console Gaming
ANIMATION AND CGI	

Table: 1.1.2 Types of Programmable Systems

1.1.2 Integrating processes with a GPU

A graphics card is a processor specifically designed to manipulate graphical information. It is integrated into the computer to prepare data before being sent to the input output system. Graphics processing units work by offloading tasks from the central processing unit, enhancing an applications performance. For instance, a computer operating at a standard clock speed may experience delays when loading data for coordinates and rendered objects, significantly slowing down processing time. In contrast, GPUs efficiently manage these tasks within a single frame.

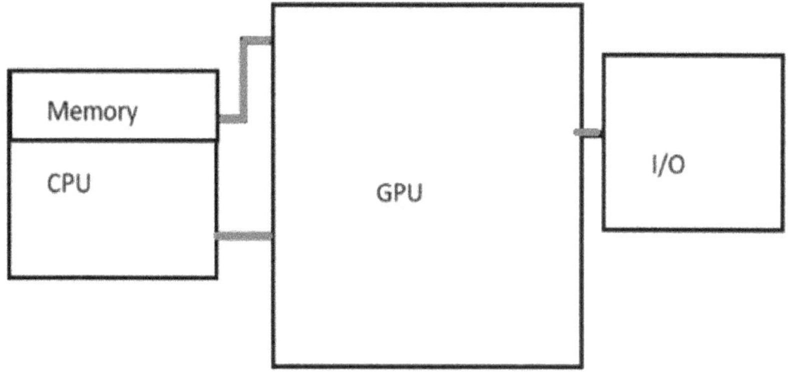

Fig: 1.1.2 the stages within the graphics pipeline.

The purpose of the GPU is to share tasks involving image processing and calculations. This reduces the time it takes to complete a program and improves the overall performance of the software. The GPU itself is designed around several cores that can conduct multiple tasks simultaneously. These are able to interpret, modify, and perform calculations on large amounts of data. The GPU also uses an expanded memory to load data between frames. This allows the shader and texture information to be stored within the cache and be retrieved anytime within the program. The events that occur within the GPU during a program's runtime are called the graphics pipeline.

1.2.1 Understanding the Graphics Pipeline

The GPU is designed to handle the movement of 3D coordinates as well as add texture and shade to the shapes. This is achieved via a number of processes that take the geometric coordinates and repopulate these inside a 3D space. The GPU prepares the graphical information before being output to the I/O. The entire procedure is called the graphics pipeline and allows the computer to step through each task producing the finished 3D image. This procedure can be broken down into several parts that contain a geometric and rendering element. This is due to the order in which the program needs to occur, as well as the structure found inside the GPU.

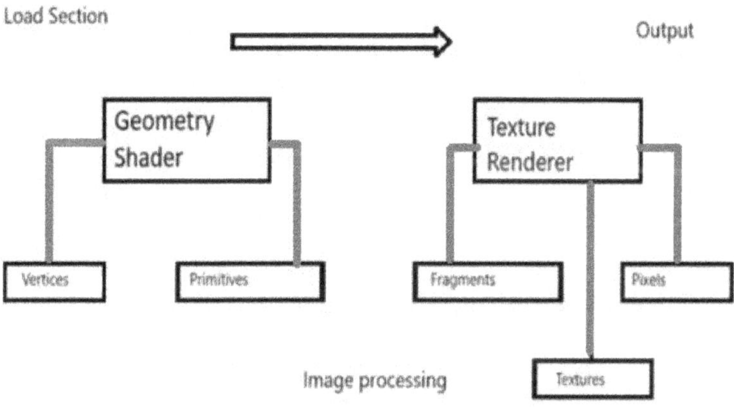

Fig: 1.2.1 the stages of the graphics pipeline.

The graphics pipeline consists of a number of stages and begins when the graphical data is loaded into the buffer, preparing the information for the program's events. This includes the coordinates for shapes and objects, as well as the textures that are applied at the end of the process. This approach allows the program to store the necessary graphical data within the GPU's memory. This loading occurs between each frame or whenever the GPU is requested to refresh its buffer. Due to the large file sizes of geometric data and texture maps, this method alleviates some of the workload on the CPU. For example, data used for shading and colouring objects can be kept in the GPU until it is no longer needed by the program. In this context, the CPU requests the GPU to handle the parts of the program that requires the modifications for the graphical elements.

1.2.2 Other purposes of the graphics pipeline

The graphics pipeline consists of a number of stages that manipulate and render the geometric coordinates. For instance, the worldview and camera position need to be constantly updated, and this is completed inside the graphics pipeline. Other processes, such as perspective projection and applying light and shadow, also occur during this stage. These again need to be completed within the GPU as the processor is responsible for any data that handles graphical information.

STAGES OF THE GRAPHICS PIPELINE	
GEOMETRIC TRANSFORMS	World coordinates
TEXTURE RENDERING	Camera position
LIGHT AND SHADOW	Clipping
PROJECTION	Image processing

Table: 1.2.3 Stages of the graphics pipeline.

1.3.1 Exploring the pipeline procedure within the GPU

Despite the many functions that the GPU commits to within the graphical pipeline. The process can be seen as having two distinct parts. The first is the coordination of the vertices and how the objects appear on screen in terms of the perspective from the camera. The second occurs in the fragment shader where the vertices are shaded and coloured. This is a very simplified version of how the GPU is expected to work but allows a better explanation of how the structures occur within the GPU. The stages are completed in a number of steps that allow the GPU to coordinate the parts of the program, prepare the geometric data, and render the coordinates after processing. This allows each part of the graphics pipeline to work in sequence.

1.3.1 Creating an object out of geometric coordinates

To better understand how the geometric calculations work, it is necessary to look at how a mesh or model is created within a program and how the GPU recognizes coordinates. Within 3D programming, a series of conventions determines how a model appears geometrically. For instance, the manipulation of 3D space uses a coordinate system to identify the location of each object. This means providing a set of coordinates to create an object along a series of axes. Here, the object has to be drawn as set points within an XYZ location. These points are known as vectors and describe their location within the grid. Vectors are used to describe both the 3D location as well as the 2D projected image.

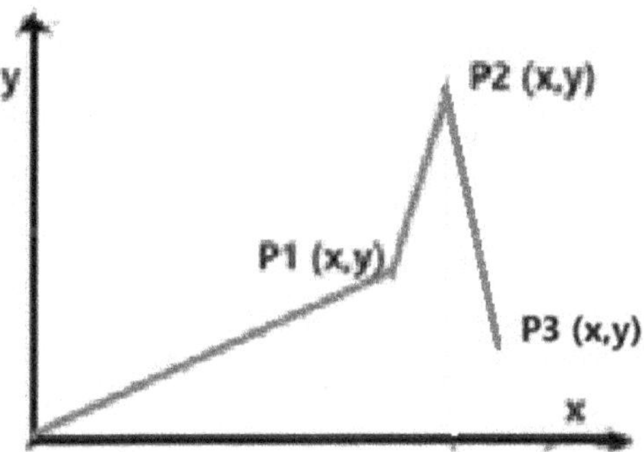

Fig: 1.3.1 Vectors as a coordinate system.

Generally, a vector can be used to describe a point within a grid or the distance between two points. For instance, a grid may start at a reference point (0,0), where a shape projected onto the grid occurs within the following locations.

Coordinates for a square

A = (2,1)
B = (5,1)
C = (2,5)
D = (5,5)

These points refer to a square captured within an XY coordinate system with a reference point of (0,0). This allows the program to identify a starting point for the object and the points along the grid to which it refers. If the object moves location, a new set of coordinates can be provided that moves the entire shape to a new position within the grid.

For instance, if the square moves 5 places along the x-axis, a new set of vector coordinates will be used to describe the location.

A = (2,1)
B = (5,1)
C = (7,5)
D = (10,5)

This example demonstrates how to plot an object as a set of points or vector coordinates within a grid or mesh. The vector will refer to the distance away from the starting location such as (0,0). Within a 3D space, the vector has three coordinates again using XYZ as the points reference. Creating an object or model means producing a group of three-point vectors.

1.3.2 Preparing coordinate data

The processor is used to change and manipulate coordinates during a program. This may be the local map size or various items held within 3D space. The GPU has a series of cores to perform this function, each with its own set of registers. These are used to store the geometric data for events that occur onscreen. Any movement or rotation during run time changes the data held within the registers. This type of design allows for more information to be held onscreen at any time. A program may change information for the coordinates in several ways. For instance, an object may move along an axis, rotate, or be rescaled into a new size. These changes to the information held within the registers create a series of calculations that repositions the coordinate before it is reflected in the I/O.

For instance, an object moving along the X-axis would mean that the first position of a three-point vector will either increase or decrease. Depending on the direction the object is facing.

Vector = (x,y,z)
Current vector = (5,2,3)
New vector = (10,2,3)

Suppose we look at this function in ASM for moving an object five paces. The program would look like the following.

```
Vector = (5,2,3)
Vector2 = (5,0,0)
_start:
mov dh, vector        ; first vector
mov de, vector2       ; second vector
mov dx, result        ; Pointer to result vector
mov cx, length / 2    ; Number of elements (16-bit values)
add_loop:
low                   ; Load vector into AX
add ax, [de]          ; Add vector2
store                 ; Store result vector
add dh, 2             ; Move to vector2
loop add_loop         ; Repeat for each word
```

This is a simple function that reflects the movement of a vector. Within a program, multiple vectors may need to be changed simultaneously. This is done in a similar way to the ASM program, except the ALU will calculate the data across hundreds of registers. The GPU completes this process using a special type of register called an AVX or MMX register and is used when multiple data sets need to be processed at once.

1.3.3 Projecting a 3D to 2D image

Projecting an image in 2D is another stage of the graphical pipeline. It is the process of changing the 3D vector into a flat picture. This occurs when the screen image presented by the GPU is calculated as an XY coordinate. Here, the original vector describing the mesh or model is recalculated to create a 2D perspective. To achieve this, the coordinates representing the model are passed through an algorithm that reformulates the object's depth inside a 2D plane. Without the geometry shader, the image would fail to project onto the screen in a 3-dimensional form. This process occurs after the GPU manipulates the objects coordinates. The shader first adjusts each object for movement or rotation before repopulating the environment within a 2D space.

For instance,
Original vector = (XYZ)
After projection = (XY)

The new 2 coordinate vector represents how the point appears after projection onto a 2D plane. The vector has to be recalculated to create a perspective along 2 axes or dimensions. The CPU can complete the calculation to achieve 2D projection and is merely a series of mathematical formulas that translate the vector by determining the distance to the Z axis. This calculation is responsible for the effect of depth found within a program.

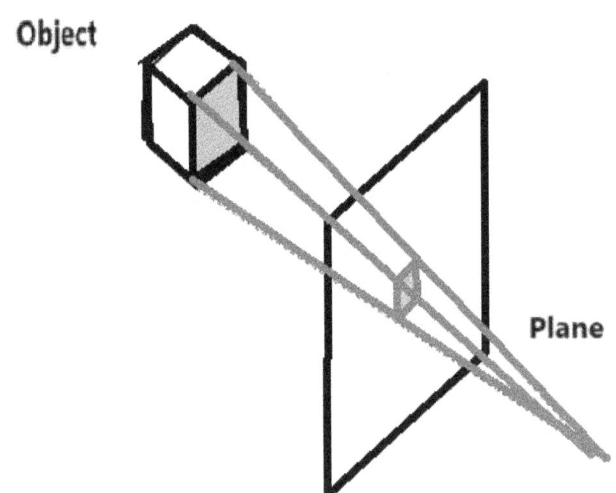

Fig: 1.3.3 Projection of a 2D image

1.4.1 Rendering the object

The final part of the graphics pipeline adjusts the geometric data, before rendering, and adding texture to the coordinates. The renderer decides how each plane is coloured and shaded according to any reference points held for each object. For instance, a colour will be added to draw each viewable polygon, drawing the polygon directly as a new colour. This process is slightly more difficult if a shader requires a texture or shadow. This is because the texture must be added to one of the memory caches and stretched onto the polygon it is drawn onto. As shapes within a 3D space change when moving, there is also a task of reformatting the texture according to the perspective and distance from the camera. The renderer has a number of techniques in which this is achieved. Several structures within the GPU are designed to calculate these differences in perspective.

As mentioned, the renderer is also where the GPU applies the light and shadow to an object. For instance, a light source may be located within the environment, casting shadows on the adjacent landscape. The fragment shader is responsible for this effect and works out the distance between a light source and any objects within the camera's viewpoint. Adapting the colour of the object present to the source of light. There are several structures within the GPU that are responsible for creating this calculation, which can simulate the presence of light and shadow within a 3D environment. The final stage of the fragment shader is to render the object onto the screen. This is the process of sending the finished 2D image to the I/O.

Summary of chapter

In this chapter, we have examined the emergence of 3D technology and how this concept is achievable within computer hardware design. The GPU is responsible for completing graphical tasks to reduce the workload of the CPU and is specifically designed to integrate and complete this process. We have also examined the graphics pipeline and the separate stages that allow the GPU to process 3D applications.

End of Chapter Quiz

List how graphic applications could improve a work sector.

Why are coordinates used above other types of data format?

Identify two computer structures found in the GPU.

Describe how a GPU might need to be designed.

CHAPTER 2

Vectors and Creating Objects

In this chapter, you will look at the following

- How coordinate systems work
- 2D and 3D planes
- Creating an object out of polygons
- Using scales and ranges

2.1.1 Using coordinates as reference points

Creating 3D environments involves developing a system to represent objects within a three-dimensional space. Coordinate systems are essential because they describe the shape and position of models and meshes. Coordinates are expressed as a set of values, which can be updated to reflect the changes in movement and rotation. This feature makes them ideal for programming virtual environments. A common approach to managing 3D data is by using vectors. These vectors indicate the location of an object relative to a point of origin; this is represented by the coordinates (0, 0, 0). For example, two objects can be positioned in space based on their respective 3D vector coordinates.

For instance, two cubes might occur at points;
First cube = (2,3,5)
Second cube = (10,5,4)

The two cubes have a position or location on a 3D grid and are moved five units along the z-axis.

First cube = (2,3,10)
Second cube = (10,5,9)

Here, the position used to describe the two cubes has been altered due to the movement along the z-axis. During a program, this event will need to occur many times under several conditions. For example, the rotation of a camera or rescaling a group of polygons will all result in a change to the object's coordinates. Creating the objects within the 3D space as a set of vectors allows the program to easily update and manipulate the object's location as needed.

2.1.2 2D and 3D coordinate systems

A standard convention used within programming coordinate systems is to portray each set of axes as a list of separate integers. Here, each axis has its point within the list. Any change to the axis within the coordinate will affect the reflected integer. This convention can be used in many programs, as modern GPUs are designed to run this type of pattern. For this reason, understanding how the coordinate system works is essential in designing graphics hardware. Put simply, the coordinate system is used to identify a point that exists within a given space.

There are two types of coordinates used in programming for three dimensions. One is used for a 2D plane, and the other for 3D. The same convention is used to write each vector type and can be used interchangeably within a program. The vectors merely state the point across each given axis.

For example, a 2D plane is written as a vector.
New vector = (x,y)

The vector represents the points along the x and y axis and is used to populate a 2D plane or projected image. Writing a vector for 3D point is quite similar, except the vector includes a third axis used to depict a z-plane.

For example, a 3D coordinate can be written as a vector.
New 3Dvector = (x,y,z)

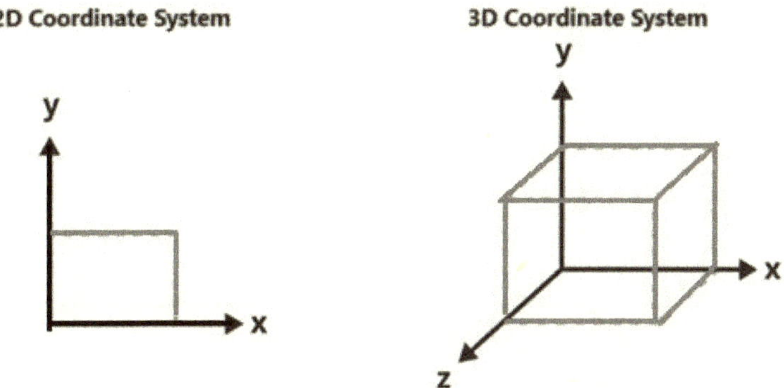

Fig: 2.1.2 The 2D and 3D coordinate axis.

2.1.3 How are coordinate systems used

In 3D programming, coordinates specify a point's distance from a reference location. Just like points defined on an x and y axes, it is possible to determine the position of a coordinate within a 3D grid. Plotting a 3D coordinate is a process of determining the vector's distance to the point of origin of the grid's axis. For example, the following vector describes a random point occurring within a three-dimensional space.

randomPoint1 = (5,0,5)

This vector indicates the distance each value occurs from the point of origin of the grid, given a starting point of (0,0,0). This technique is used to locate any vector used within a program. It is possible to draw this point on the grid, which would look like the following on a chart.

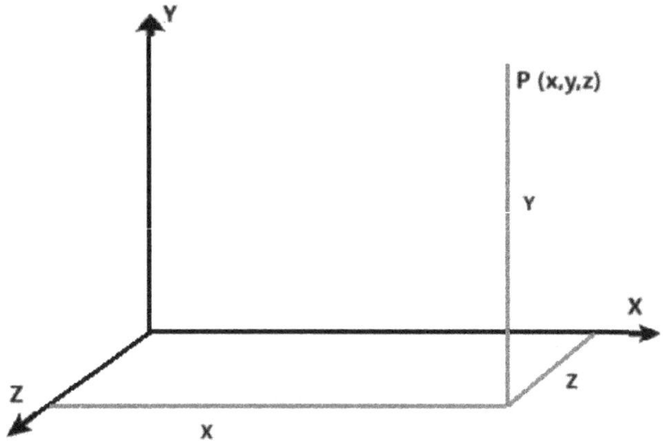

Fig: 2.1.3 Plotting a 3D coordinate

2.4.1 Expressing ranges and scales

Scales and ranges are used to describe the ratio and size of objects within their environment. For instance, several cubes may be placed in a virtual environment with a series of coordinates 5 units away from each other. The purpose of identifying the ratio of objects to their environment allows the programmer to recognize how the coordinate might appear once on screen. For instance, a unit within an environment might be ten points apart, allowing the programmer to design the shape within these typical parameters.

A range merely indicates how many units are available within the environment and where an object might be located within a given space. Below is a series of vectors using different scales.

newVectorl = (5,5,5), (10,10,10), (15,15,15)
newVector2 = (25,25,25), (50,50,50), (75,75,75)
newVector3 = (100,100,100), (200,200,200), (300,300,300)

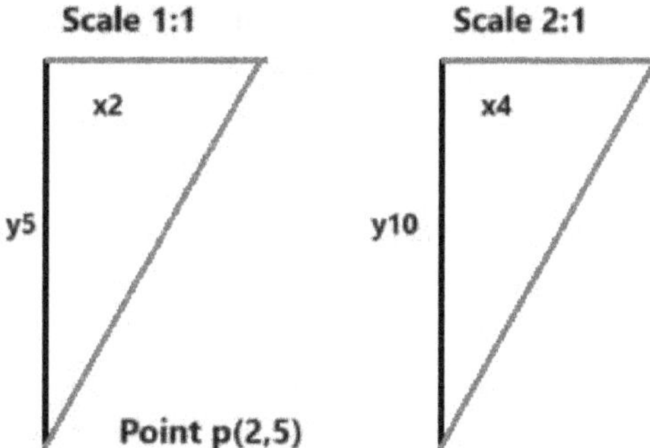

Fig:2.4.1 Description of two coordinates using different scalars

2.2.1 Creating a 2D shape

Despite being ordinarily used to plot graphs, a 2D grid can be used to plot a number of points along the x and y axes. For instance, it is possible to plot a set of points as either x and y coordinates to represent a square. This could be written into a program that would draw a square across the axis. Below is an example of how to write the code to simulate this.

```
import matplotlib.pyplot as plt
# Coordinates of the square
square = [
    (1, 1), (1, 2),
    (2, 2), (2, 1),
    (1, 1) # Closing the square]

# Unzip coordinates
x, y = zip(*square)

# Plot the square
plt.figure() plt.plot(x, y, marker='o')
plt.title('Square along X and Y Axis')
plt.xlabel('X Axis')
plt.ylabel('Y Axis')
plt.grid(True)
plt.gca().set_aspect('equal'adjustable='box')
```

The coordinates within the grid can represent points within a square. This technique can also be applied to create larger items and even 3D images by identifying the points that define a shape. For example, constructing a mesh involves arranging multiple polygons side by side until they resemble the shape and volume of an object. This process requires determining how the structure can be represented as a series of polygons.

ADVANTAGES OF USING COORDINATE SYSTEMS	
2D OR 3D APPLICATIONS	Reduces complex code
IDENTIFICATION OF POINTS	Transformation and recalculation
SCALE AND RANGE	projection
RENDERING AN OBJECT	Data concerns

Table: 2.2.1 Advantages of coordinate systems

2.2.2 Designing objects using vector coordinates

Creating a 3D object is similar to drawing a shape on a 2D plane, except the points are written as a set of 3D coordinates. The object will comprise of a series of points that indicate their position from the point of origin. These points represent the vectors used to draw the model. Once these vectors are identified, it's possible to draw the object by connecting the relevant coordinates. For example, a cube will have eight points listed as a set of vectors used to design the shape's dimensions.

The following program demonstrates how these can be plotted onto a grid to draw an eight-sided cube. As can be seen, the vertices are described before being repopulated as a series of squares to represent an 8-sided image.

```
import matplotlib.pyplot as plt
from mpl_toolkits.mplot3d.art3d import Poly3DCollection

# Define the vertices of the cube
    vertices = [
    [0, 0, 0], [1, 0, 0], [1, 1, 0], [0, 1, 0], # Bottom face
    [0, 0, 1], [1, 0, 1], [1, 1, 1], [0, 1, 1] # Top face]
```

```
# Define the edges that connect the vertices
edges = [
[vertices[0], vertices[1], vertices[2], vertices[3]], # Bottom face
[vertices[4], vertices[5], vertices[6], vertices[7]], # Top face
[vertices[0], vertices[1], vertices[5], vertices[4]], # Front face
[vertices[2], vertices[3], vertices[7], vertices[6]], # Back face
[vertices[0], vertices[3], vertices[7], vertices[4]], # Left face
[vertices[1], vertices[2], vertices[6], vertices[5]] # Right face]

# Create a 3D plot
fig = plt.figure()
ax = fig.add_subplot(111, projection='3d')

# Add the faces to the plot
poly3d = [[tuple(vertex) for vertex in face] for face in edges] ax.add_collection3d(Poly3DCollection(poly3d, facecolors='cyan', linewidths=1, edgecolors='r', alpha=.25))

# Set plot limits
ax.set_xlabel('X')
ax.set_ylabel('Y')
ax.set_zlabel('Z')
ax.set_xlim([0, 1])
ax.set_ylim([0, 1])
ax.set_zlim([0, 1])

# Show the plot
plt.show()
```

The output from the program is listed below. Here, the cube's vertices have been redrawn on the grid to reflect how an image might appear within a 3D space.

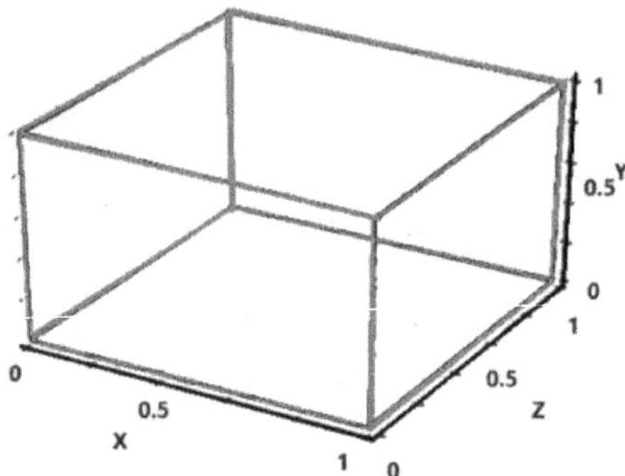

Fig: 2.1.2 a 3d projected image.

Despite the image being drawn in 3D, for most programs, the image must be redrawn onto a 2D plane using just the x and y-axis. This technique is called projection and recalculates 3 integer vertices to a 2-integer vector. To achieve this technique an image has to be recalculated several times. This will be explained in further chapters.

2.3.1 Defining planes and polygons

Polygons are a common method of creating shapes or planes for the use of designing models. The reason is that the coordinates or vertices alone will only describe the points of a shape but not how the edges are formed. As was demonstrated with the function for creating a cube. It was seen that the shape required a description of how the coordinates were joined. For instance, the program for the eight-sided cube required a method of identifying each of the cube's faces to draw the edges. This assumption is typical of creating meshes or models, as the coordinates themselves do not describe how the shape is formed. For the program to recognize the structure of the planes, coordinates can be grouped into polygons, which allows the program to draw the images in a series of 2D shapes.

Here is a simple description of a polygon, with four coordinates

(5,6)
(6,7.5)
(3,7)
(2,5)

The output for the vectors provides the following shape, although it could be redrawn in several ways. It depends on how the program intends to recognize the points within the vertices. For instance, it could be redrawn as a set of triangles.

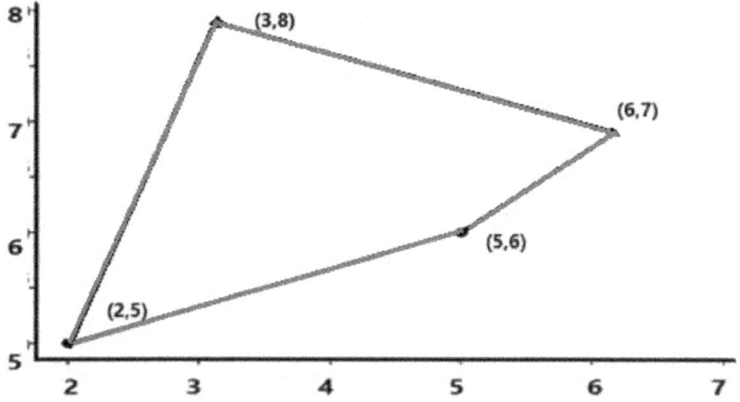

Fig: 2.3.1 A set of coordinates drawn as a four-sided polygon

For this reason, programs that use models or meshes to draw shapes require the vectors to be grouped into relevant polygons. A common pattern for drawing polygons is a series of triangles or squares, as they are simpler to form when building or designing new shapes. Most meshes can be broken down into just one set of polygons. The polygons are then drawn together to create the mesh or model. Using just one method for drawing a shape, makes it easier for the geometry shader to draw and render each plane.

For example, the following code represents a list of coordinates to draw a simple set of triangles side by side. The coordinates are listed as a 2D pattern along an XY axis.

```
# Define the edges that connect the vertices
polygons = [[[100, 300,], [300, 300,], [100, 300,]],
        [[100, 300,], [300, 500,], [300, 300,]],
        [[300, 100,], [500, 300,], [500, 300,]],
        [[300, 500,], [300, 300,], [500, 300,]],]
```

```
# Draw the edges
for i in range(len(polygons)):
        pygame.draw.line(screen, (0, 255, 255), (polygons[i][0][0], polygons[i][0][1]),(polygons[i][1][0], polygons[i][1][1]), 1)
        pygame.draw.line(screen, (0, 255, 255), (polygons[i][1][0], polygons[i][1][1]),(polygons[i][2][1], polygons[i][2][0]), 1)
        pygame.draw.line(screen, (0, 255, 255), (polygons[i][2][0], polygons[i][2][1]),(polygons[i][0][1], polygons[i][0][0]), 1)
```

How the code works is that it loops through every coordinate, drawing each triangle in turn. The algorithm represents how the geometry shader might sort the information from a list, and repopulate the values onto the screen. Here, despite being a 2D image, the principle is similar to that of a 3D shape. The concept to understand is how the program might work inside the GPU. What occurs is that each vector is read in turn, looping through the same algorithm to draw the series of shapes. As the program repeats the same process, this reduces the code and makes less of a demand on the GPU.

APPLICATIONS THAT USE VECTOR MESHES FOR MODELING	
GAMES	Geometry
DESIGN TOOLS	Facial recognition
GRAPHICS DISPLAYS	Modelling
FILMMAKING	Landscape imaging

Table: 2.3.1 Software technologies that apply vector coordinates

2.3.2 Mapping polygons and meshes

Generally, 3D images are more complex than a few polygons and are the total of several shapes put together. This means that the number of polygons used for an object may consist of 100 or more separate planes. For this reason, making the procedure to draw the shapes as simple as possible allows the processor to handle more shapes at a faster rate. For instance, a cube will only contain eight separate planes or vectors. Whereas a complex model of an imagined landscape will need many more separate planes to create the images. As we have seen, creating groups of polygons can allow an image to be drawn using a single program. Once the image is calculated, the geometry shader is responsible for processing it into a picture on the screen.

For instance below is a series of vectors to create an automobile. As can be seen this mesh contains nearly 24 coordinates. However, this is quite basic in comparison to a more detailed version, which would use many more planes to create a likeness of the shape.

```
vertices = [[0,0,0], [0,1,0], [1,0,0], [1,1,0],
            [0,0,1], [0,1,1], [1,0,1], [1,1,1],
            [-1,-1,0], [1,-1,0], [-1,1,0], [1,1,0],
            [-1,-1,-1], [1,-1,-1], [-1,1,-1], [1,1,-1],
            [-1.5,-0.5,0], [1.5,-0.5,0], [-1.5,0.5,0], [1.5,0.5,0],
            [-1.5,-0.5,-0.5], [1.5,-0.5,-0.5], [-1.5,0.5,-0.5], [1.5,0.5,-0.5]]
```

In fact, it is possible to create objects with thousands of vectors on the GPU at any given time. For example, writing the format for a simple teapot can take over four thousand vectors to describe some of the curvatures within the shape's geometry. Due to the potential combinations of vectors within a 3D environment, some object files are very complex, and it is possible to draw any number of shapes using this type of procedure.

Summary of chapter

This chapter has identified some of the types of data that are used to create objects within the geometry shader. The main intention of the chapter was to explore how vertices are used to position coordinates for models within a 3D environment. The chapter has also explored how polygons are used within a program to create the planes used to design the shape of the object. These are two important concepts as they are used not only in terms of the application's hardware, but also for rendering textures applied to the polygons once on screen.

End of Chapter Quiz

What structure in the GPU is used to transform vertices?

Why are coordinate systems used to plot points on an XYZ axis?

List several ways in which polygons can be used for rendering.?

Describe the functions the geometry shader is used for.

CHAPTER 3

Rotation and movement

In this chapter, you will look at the following

- Concepts of basic movement
- Theory of mathematical transforms
- Algorithms used for movement and rotation
- Coding the ALU and ASM

3.1.1 Concepts of basic movement

The geometry shader is responsible for processing the data used to describe a vector or coordinate. Within a program the geometry shader is responsible for the transform of the objects' position and location. The two most common types of transforms occur within the movement or rotation of an object. A transform is achieved by obtaining the current location and changing the values referring to the points axis. Using a set of vectors to plot objects allows any of the points within the vector to be manipulated, as each point has a separate value to state the point along the axis. Several procedures are used to recalculate a coordinate, depending on the type of transform that is being completed. These types of calculations apply to not only movement but also 2D projection, camera position, and the manipulation of the world map.

TYPES OF PROCESSES COMPLETED BY THE GEOMETRY SHADER	
TRANSFORMS	Camera movement
ROTATION	Addition
PROJECTION TO 2D	Subtraction
MANIPULATIONS OF WORLD MAP	Triangular formulas

Table: 3.1.1 Mathematical processes used by the geometry shader

3.1.2 Calculations involving movement along an axis

As we have seen changing the position of the object within a set of coordinates is achieved by updating the integer, corresponding to the axis of movement. As a general rule of vector coordinates, the x-axis represents the horizontal angle and the y-axis represents the vertical. For instance, an object moving vertically on the Y axis would be achieved using the following vector transform.

newVectorl = (2,0,3)
Move vertical 5
newVvectorl = (2,5,3)

A similar procedure occurs if the shape moves along the horizontal or X-axis.

newVectorl = (2,0,3)
Move horizontal 5
newVvectorl = (7,0,3)

This would produce the following output if these two vectors were drawn onto a 2D grid.

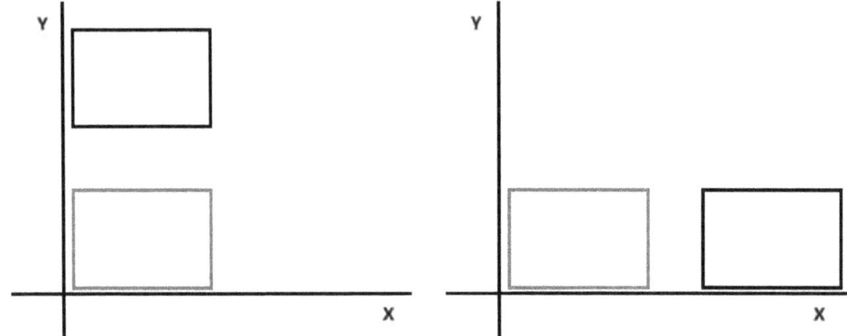

Fig: 3.1.2 Changing the axis within a coordinate.

Transforming a vector allows an object to be repositioned within a 3D space. Once the coordinates are passed through the geometry shader the new position of the object will be projected to reflect the change in the vector's coordinates. For instance, changing the x or y coordinates will create the perception of moving the object up, down, or horizontally. This can be achieved in several ways within the program. A common method is to create a while loop, which applies a transform to each vector.

The following code demonstrates how an application might reposition a set of coordinates if moved horizontally.

```
# Function to move vertices horizontally
def move_vertices_horizontally(vertices, distance):
    moved_vertices = []
    for vertex in vertices:
        x, y, z = vertex
        moved_vertex = (x + distance, y, z)
        moved_vertices.append(moved_vertex)
    return moved_vertices

# Example
vertices = [(1, 2, 3), (4, 5, 6), (7, 8, 9)]
distance = 2 # Distance to move along the X-axis
moved_vertices = move_vertices_horizontally(vertices, distance)

print("Original vertices:", vertices)
print("Moved vertices:", moved_vertices)
```

As can be seen, the code takes each vector in turn and creates a new coordinate from the vector. Altering the x coordinate to reflect the movement along the axis.

3.1.3 Movement along the vertical and horizontal planes

A plane refers to a coordinate that consists of 2 axes, such as the horizontal or vertical planes. Providing a coordinate as a plane allows the vector to be referenced separately from the remaining axis. By identifying which plane the object's position refers to, it can be moved freely within a two-dimensional space. Within 3D programming, these types of transformations restrict the movement across one axis so that the object can be carefully repositioned. For instance, a cube moving above a horizontal plane will only move within the x and z axis, restricting the movement within the vertical plane. This allows the object to move in any direction within the designated parameters.

Here is a series of 2D planes indicating which axis the coordinates refer to.

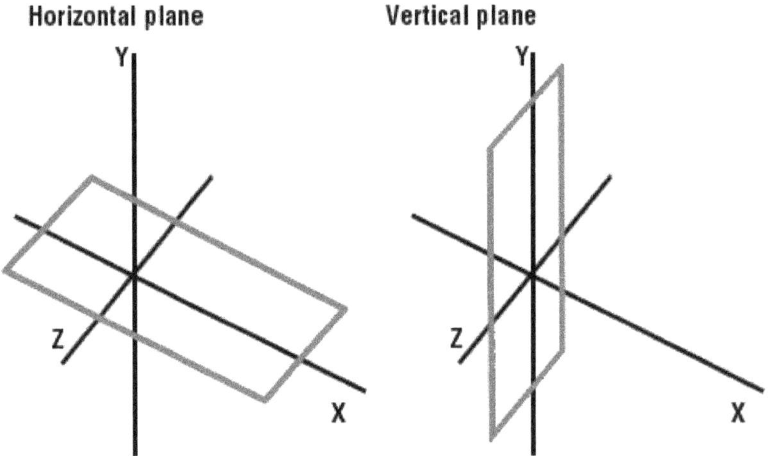

Fig: 3.1.3 The horizontal and vertical planes

As can be seen from the diagram, a 3D axis can be rewritten as a series of 2D planes. By replacing one axis with a constant the entire plane can move freely within the other coordinates. This technique is also proper when changing the shape of an object or determining its depth or range.

Here is an example of a program that can alter two values within a three-point vector so that movement is only completed across a 2D plane.

```
def transform_horizontal_plane(vectors, dx, dy):
    transformed_vectors = vectors.copy()
    transformed_vectors[:, 0] += dx # Update X coordinates
    transformed_vectors[:, 1] += dy # Update Y coordinates
    return transformed_vectors
```

```
# Example usage
vectors = np.array([
    [2, 3, 4],
    [5, 6, 7],
    [8, 9, 10]])
dx = 1
dy = 2

transformed_vectors = transform_horizontal_plane(vectors, dx, dy)

print("Original Vectors:")
print(vectors)
print("Transformed Vectors:")
print(transformed_vectors)
```

3.2.1 Rotations of coordinates

Rotation is another method of transforming the integers within a set of vectors so that it reflects the camera movement, or rotation of an object in 3D space. For instance, if an object moves between two points and turns around a 90-degree angle. The vector used to describe the object will have changed orientation. Rotation accounts for a major proportion of the processes that the ALU performs and requires several mathematical functions to complete a simple reposition of vectors. The principle behind rotation works similarly to movement, as the coordinates are repositioned through a mathematical function before being repopulated within the worldview. The difference is that rotation takes several processes to achieve and requires slightly more mathematical functions to rework a vector into a new set of geometric data.

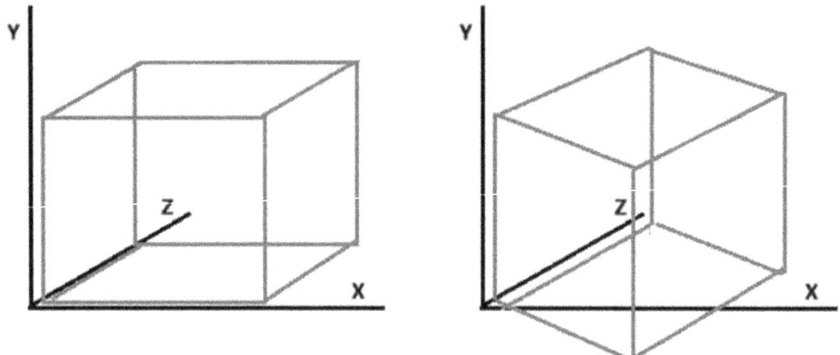

Fig: 3.2.1 An object rotating around a fixed point

3.2.2 Creating a Simple Rotation Matrix

The function used for rotation can be used in any number of procedures where a coordinate rotates around a single point. What occurs is that each vector is transformed through a matrix so that the coordinate reflects the new angle. This can be represented mathematically as a simple algebraic expression where each axis is processed in turn through a separate formula. The product of the calculation provides the result of the transformation.

Below is a matrix to determine a simple rotation along the X-axis

[Xpp] = [1, 0, 0] = [Xp]
[Ypp] [0, cos(Rx), -sin(Rx)] [Yp]
[Zpp] [0, sin(Rx), cos(Rx)] [Zp]

Here the original vector Xpp is recalculated as a new set of coordinates Xp. The value for the angle is given as Rx and indicates the angle of reflection around the X-axis. Within a 3D environment, each vector used to describe an object will go through the same transform to reiterate the points held for each vector. This performs the process of perceiving the object at a new angle.

Here are the matrices again for rotations referring to the remaining axis.

Y-axis

[Xpp] = [cos(Ry), 0, sin(Ry)] = [Xp]
[Ypp] [0, 1, 0)] [Yp]
[Zpp] [-sin(Ry), 0, cos(Ry)] [Zp]

Z axis

[Xpp] = [cos(Rz), -sin(Rz), 0] = [Xp]
[Ypp] [sin(Rz), sin(Rz), 0] [Yp]
[Zpp] [0,0, 1] [Zp]

As can be seen, the formulas themselves are similar and achieve the same basis of rotation. A point to note is that the formula is dependent on which axis and angle the function refers to.

3.2.3 Writing a rotation as a program

As we have seen the rotation transform requires a formula to recalculate the coordinates. This formula is also used when writing the code to manipulate sets of data within a program. Here a single function is dependent on which type of rotation is being called. For instance, a rotation along the vertical axis requires a separate function from the horizontal transform. Below is a program to identify how this process is completed.

```
import numpy as np

def rotate_x(vector, angle):
 # Convert angle from degrees to radians
 angle_rad = np.radians(angle)

 # Define the rotation matrix for rotation around the x-axis
 rotation_matrix = np.array([
   [1, 0, 0],
   [0, np.cos(angle_rad), -np.sin(angle_rad)],
   [0, np.sin(angle_rad), np.cos(angle_rad)]])
```

```
# Apply the rotation matrix to the vector
rotated_vector = np.dot(rotation_matrix, vector)
return rotated_vector

# Example usage
vector = np.array([1, 0, 0])
angle = 45 # Rotate by 45 degrees
rotated_vector = rotate_x(vector, angle)
print("Rotated Vector:", rotated_vector)
```

As can be seen, the program uses the rotation matrix to recalculate any of the vectors used to describe an object. Depending on which axis the object rotates around, the program used to describe the rotation will be written using a different set of formulas with separate sets of matrices.

3.3.1 How the processor completes transformations

The arithmetic unit is responsible for manipulating the data that flows through the geometry shader. Any transformations applied to a point vector are executed by the arithmetic logic unit (ALU). This specialized component can recalculate data using various formulas and logical comparisons. During a program's execution, data for a given set of points is loaded into the registers of the arithmetic unit. Depending on the process, a series of calculations can convert the data from one set of coordinates to a new transformed set. This transformation occurs for various events within a program, such as camera movement, projection, and rotation. To carry out these procedures, the ALU has several structures and circuits to reinterpret the binary data stored in the unit's registers.

The structure of the ALU within the graphics card is designed similarly to the one found in a computer's processor; however, the GPU contains many more cores, each with its own ALU. This design is necessary to process large data sets simultaneously under various conditions. As a result, the GPU is able to process larger amounts of graphical data to the processor found in the GPU.

EXAMPLE CALCULATION PERFORMED BY ALU	
ADD	Compare
SUBTRACT	Logical functions
INCREMENT	AND, OR, NOT
DECREMENT	Shift

Table: 3.1.1 Mathematical processes used by the geometry shader

3.3.2 Transformation of a vector using ASM

To better understand the functions of the ALU and how the core works between calculations. Writing the code as a series of ASM routines explains how each process is possible. The reason is that ASM is similar to machine language and better describes how the core is expected to move information between registers during each stage of a single calculation.

For example, an object is positioned at a starting vector and moves along the x-axis 5 coordinates to produce a new vector.

```
newVectorl = (2,0,5)
add vector (0,5,0)
newVectorl = (2,5,5)
```

Here the starting point is (2,0,5) and moves along the axis in 5 units. The code repositioning the coordinates might appear like the code written below. This would be used each time the program expects to move along any given axis. The program merely takes two sets of vectors and adds the coordinates, to produce a new output. This function is often called during a program, which can produce movement across any axis. For example, the code might appear when repositioning or moving an object's location. The program would be used to transform any given set of vectors.

```
section .data
 vectors dw 2, 3, 4, ; Vector 1 (x1, y1, z1)
    dw 5, 6, 7, ; Vector 2 (x2, y2, z2)
    dw 8, 9, 10 ; Vector 3 (x3, y3, z3)
add_value dw 1 ; Value to add to each coordinate
```

```
section .bss
   result resw 9 ; Storage for the resulting vectors

section .text
   global _start

_start:
   mov esi, vectors ; Pointer to the vectors array
   mov edi, result ; Pointer to the result array
   mov ecx, 9 ; Number of coordinates (3 vectors x 3 coordinates each)
   mov ax, [add_value] ; Load the value to add

add_loop:
   mov bx, [esi] ; Load coordinate from vector
   add bx, ax ; Add the value
   mov [edi], bx ; Store the result
   add esi, 2 ; Move to the next coordinate in the vector array
   add edi, 2 ; Move to the next coordinate in the result array
   loop add_loop

   ; Exit the program
   mov eax, 1 ; syscall: exit
   xor ebx, ebx ; exit code 0
   int 0x80 ; interrupt to invoke syscall
```

The program loads the vectors for the location and movement into two separate registers. Once the coordinates are inside the ALU it is possible to add the contents of the register to each of the values for the vector. The program then continues to loop through any further points for the object. This describes how the processor within the geometry shader expects to work through a set of data. The processor moves the information into ALU before recalculating the group of points. This procedure is similar to other functions used for transformation, such as rotation and camera movement, as the core, steps through a number of stages that manipulate the contents of the vector's coordinates.

Here is the process used to calculate a rotation.

```
; Apply rotation around the Z-axis
; x' = x * cos(angle) - y * sin(angle)
; y' = x * sin(angle) + y * cos(angle)
fld dword [angle_rad] ; Load angle in radians
fsincos ; Compute cos(angle) and sin(angle)
; cos(angle) -> st(0)
; sin(angle) -> st(1)
fxch st(1) ; Exchange st(0) and st(1) so sin(angle) is on top

; x' = x * cos(angle) - y * sin(angle)
fmul st(0), st(2) ; x * sin(angle)
fmul st(1), st(3) ; y * cos(angle)
fsub st(1), st(0) ; x' = x * cos(angle) - y * sin(angle)
fstp dword [edi] ; Store x'

; y' = x * sin(angle) + y * cos(angle)
fld dword [angle_rad] ; Reload angle in radians
fsincos ; Recompute cos(angle) and sin(angle)
fxch st(1) ; Exchange st(0) and st(1) so sin(angle) is on top
fmul st(0), st(2) ; x * sin(angle)
fmul st(1), st(3) ; y * cos(angle)
faddp st(1), st(0) ; y' = x * sin(angle) + y * cos(angle)
fstp dword [edi + 2] ; Store y'

; Store the original z value (unchanged)
fild word [esi + 4] ; Load z
fistp dword [edi + 4] ; Store z'
```

Here, each value from the three-point vector is recalculated in a series of functions that mimic how the matrix for rotation is expected to work. The result for the new vector then replaces the vector that was currently held to describe the point's location. This example program describes the types of processes that the GPU completes each time a set of data passes through the geometry shader. As the processor has many cores, these functions happen simultaneously across many data sets. Allowing the program to simulate and move multiple objects within 3D space.

3.5.1 Rotation of an object in model-view

The rotation of an object relies on the formula to move each coordinate around the centre of its location. This type of procedure differs from moving multiple objects, as this is achieved via rotation of the world map. Instead, when an object still intends to retain its original position, the location of the object needs to remain intact. For this reason, the object's centre must be identified when rotating the coordinates. Here, the coordinates that refer to the object's points can be listed as either positive or negative in reference to the centre. This allows the formula to differentiate if the point is turning towards the centre or away.

For instance, the following set of coordinates refers to the points within an eight-sided cube. The points are not scaled but allow for a set of vertices that can determine the cube's edges.

```
vertices = [
[1, 1, -1], [1, -1, -1], [-1, -1, -1],
[-1, 1, -1], [1, 1, 1], [1, -1, 1],
[-1, -1, 1], [-1, 1, 1]]
```

The output might look like the following once drawn to a scale, and the coordinates within the vertices are identified.

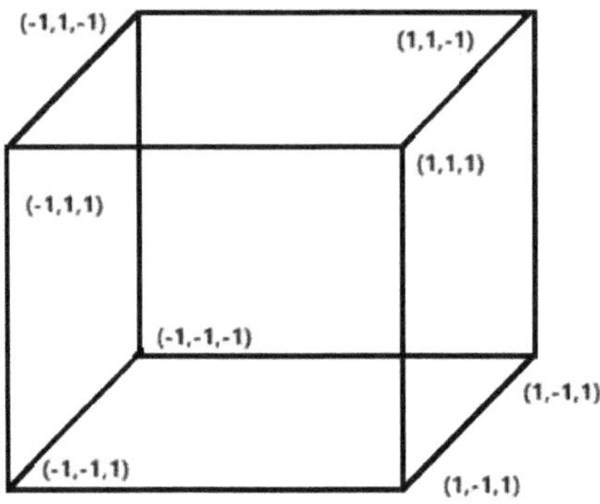

Fig:3.5.1 A cube listed within a rotatable grid

Identifying the points within the cube allows the program to turn each vector in the correct direction each time the rotation procedure is called.

Without identifying the points of a rotating object, each coordinate would move in the same direction as if rotating around a separate position.

Below is an example of how this might appear within a program.

```
x = [-1,1,1,-1,-1,1,1,-1]
y = [-1,-1,1,1,-1,-1,1,1]
z = [1,1,1,1,-1,-1,-1,-1]

#global coordinates
xg = [0,1,2,3,4,5,6,7]
yg = [0,1,2,3,4,5,6,7]
zg = [0,1,2,3,4,5,6,7]

scale = 200
pos = 300

def rotate(angle):
  for i in range(len(x)):
    a = [x[i], y[i], z[i]]
    b = [cos(angle), 0, sin(angle)]
    xpp = np.inner(a,b)
    b = [0, 1, 0]
    ypp = np.inner(a,b)
    b = [-sin(angle), 0, cos(angle)]
    zpp = np.inner(a,b)
    [xg[i], yg[i], zg[i]] = [xpp*scale+pos, ypp*scale+pos, zpp*scale+pos]
    print (x[i],y[i],z[i])
```

As can be seen, this program allows the rotation formula to move the coordinates toward the centre. Without a series of reference points, the rotation would turn each coordinate in the same direction.

Summary of chapter

The chapter aimed to identify how coordinates can be recalculated to provide transforms that reflect basic procedures such as movement and rotation. Many types of software need to reposition models and meshes during design or create a realistic and lifelike movement. For this reason, a set of rules determines how data held as coordinates can be recalculated to mimic different types of change or movement.

End of Chapter Quiz

List several uses of vector transforms.

Describe how a program simulates movement.

How does rotation differ from other types of transforms?

What part of the GPU recalculates data held as vectors?

CHAPTER 4

Projection onto a 2D plane

In this chapter, you will look at the following

- Identifying the 2D projection plane
- Changing 3D coordinates to XY
- Mathematical concepts to create perspective
- Creating an algorithm

4.1.1 Perspective as a programming concept

A lot like how it is possible to judge a sense of distance in our environment, programming in 3D space uses a similar set of principles to create perspective. For instance, the scale of an object determines the distance something might be from the horizon, as well as the perception of depth visible at a given angle. These points of reference indicate that an object has three dimensions. When the camera moves around the object, it is possible to visualize these differences. To complete this process a series of techniques are used to portray the movement between the coordinate's vectors and the distance projected onto a 2D plane. This allows a program to produce a 2D image with a sense of perspective. During a program the object will be recalculated a number of times to allow for the alterations of movement and rotation. These will also be reflected within other elements within the program such as the projection of the environment within the 2D plane.

For example, scale is a regular indication of the distance an object might appear from a given point. An object's size diminishes if it is moved away from the camera and increases if the camera approaches its centre. This effect creates a sense of perspective as it is possible to distinguish where in the environment the two objects occur. This can be seen in the image below as the two cubes can be perceived at different locations according to their scale and position on the horizon.

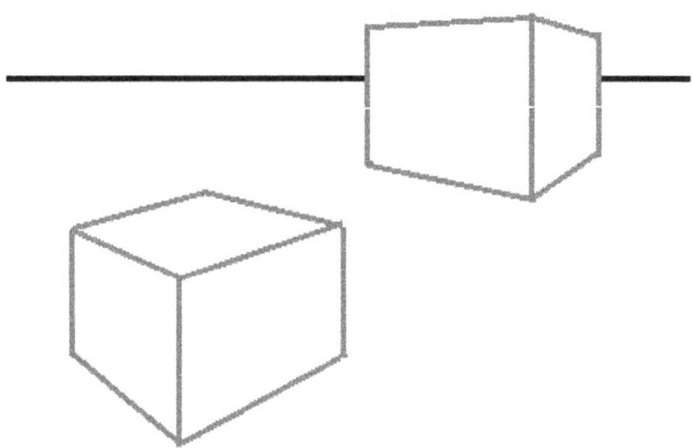

Fig: 4.1.1 Two cubes in perspectives

A similar sense of judgement is achieved when applying this rule to the depth of an image, where the points of the object produce a reduction in scale according to the distance from the viewing angle. To create the perspective within a program, the coordinates, which define a set of points for a model, must be recalculated to project the image onto a 2D plane. A lot like the procedure for transformations and movement. The projection of the images is achieved through a series of mathematical formulas.

HOW DO WE JUDGE 3D AND PERSPECTIVE?	
SCALE/DEPTH	Light and shadow
DISTANCE	Speed of movement
VANISHING POINT	Detail and texture
BINOCULAR DISPARITY	Similarity to other objects

Table: 3.1.1 Mathematical processes used by the geometry shader

4.1.2 Field of view and 2D projection

Projection of the 2D image within a program can be achieved by identifying the perspective of the objects shape. Here, the position of a camera is used to create a viewing angle that determines how the coordinates are perceivable from any one starting point or location. The coordinates that describe the 3D vectors are redetermined onto a 2D plane to allow for the difference in perspective. The camera can redefine the image as a new set of vectors that define the distance of the objects shape.

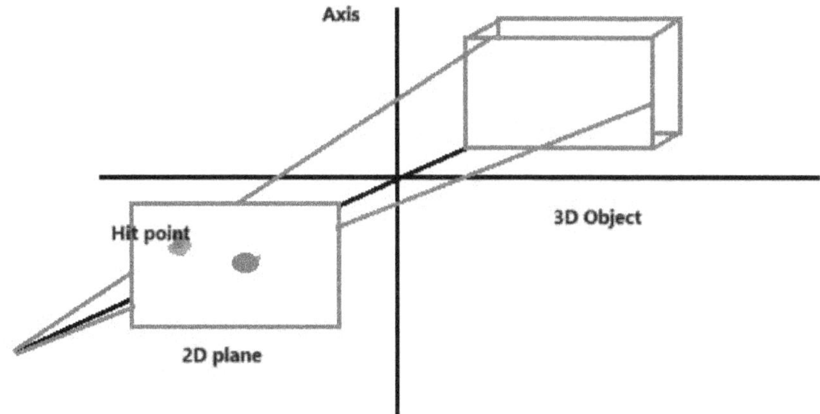

Fig:4.1.2 Projection onto a 2D plane

As can be seen from the diagram, the 2D image that is projected has a new set of coordinates that redefine the object within a single plane. Any movement of the object also creates a new set of 2D coordinates. This projection can be defined within a series of mathematical principles that determine how the (x,y) vectors are formed using the original points for the object.

4.2.1 Mathematical basis of perspective

The projection of a 3D image to a 2D plane involves recalculating the vectors given in 3 coordinates and repopulating these onto an x,y grid. Once recalculated, the finished image should appear in-depth and in perspective. This process can be determined using a series of mathematical formulas that can judge the distance of the camera to any point within the object. To explain this further it is possible to visualise, a 2D plane being placed between the camera position and the point of an object. The camera is only able to see the position of the object through the 2D plane.

This would indicate the point of the coordinate as represented within the image of a 2D display.

This can be visualized below.

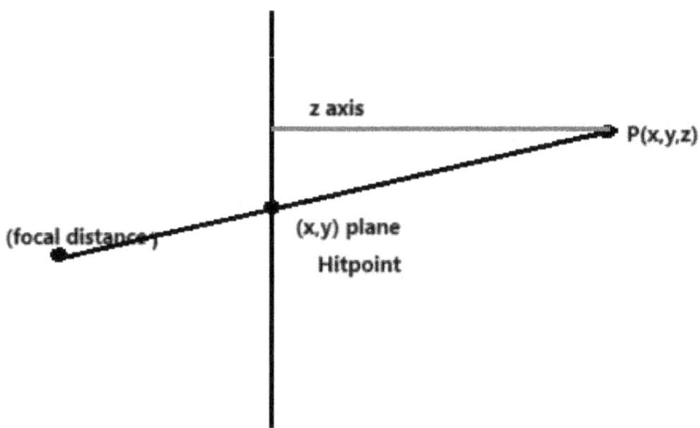

Fig: 4.2.1 Creating a hit point on a 2D plane

The three-point coordinate has been transformed into a 2D coordinate on a vertical plane. The hit point represents how the coordinates values have changed according to the distance from point P to the flat 2D plane. Once all the coordinates have been mapped, the new projection will be a 2D image.

This can be represented as an equation to obtain the new coordinates for (x,y) as they might appear on the grid.

X = distance(x)/ distance(x) + z
Y = distance(y)/ distance(y) + z

Where:

Distance(x) = x
Distance(y) = y

The distance between the two points can be obtained by finding the length between the coordinates x and z. This would obtain the focal distance as it might appear within an algorithm. This is the hypotenuse or longest side of the vectors (x,z) and (y,z). Using this formula allows the new values of the 2D projection to be calculated for a single point. This can be completed across all points within a dataset to obtain a 2D representation of an object. Effectively recalculating each point.

It is possible to use a matrix used to represent the same formula.

[x} = [factor, S, 0] = [x]
[y] [0, factor, 0] [y]
[z] [0, 0, 1] [z]

S = Skew
Factor = distance(x)/ distance(x) + z
Factor = distance(y)/ distance(y) + z

This matrix represents the same equation to judge distance. It is merely written as a product of each point. Here, the skew can be replaced with any value that improves the projection processing.

4.3.1 Creating algorithms for perspective and projection

The arithmetic used to calculate the distance of the point in 3D space can be rewritten as an algorithm to determine the projection of an object's vectors. The program works by looping through each vector in turn, until every coordinate has been recalculated to represent the change in perspective. The algorithm redefines the 3D vectors into a series of x and y coordinates, which indicate their points within a 2D plane, effectively redefining each vector.

For example, a series of vectors can describe the coordinates for each point within the cube. Here, the coordinates still retain each value for the XYZ axis.

polygons = [[-1,-1,1],[1,-1,1],[1,1,1],[-1,1,1],[-1,-1,-1],[1,-1,-1],[1,1,-1],[-1,1,-1]]

After recalculating the coordinates, a set of new vectors is obtained within the x and y axes. These can be used to determine their points within the 2D plane. Below is an example of how the new vectors might appear within just two axes.

[(477, 136), (201, 162), (201, 513), (477, 461), (280, 86), (68, 95), (68, 365), (280, 338)]

The image obtained from the output would look like the following. It is possible to determine which face of the cube appears at the front of the object.

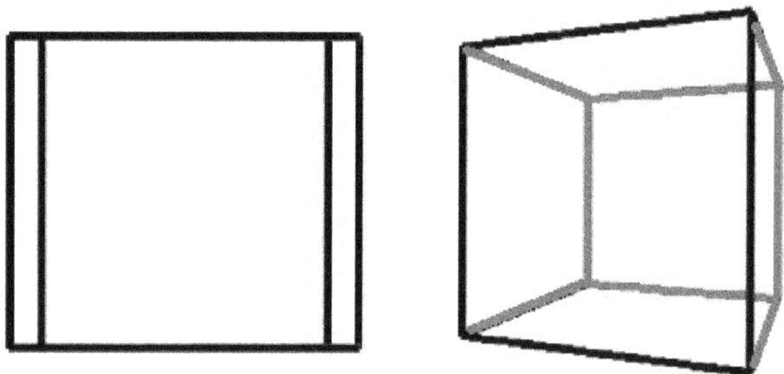

Fig: 4.3.1 2D image of the cube before and after applying perspective

As can be seen, using projection to redefine the points used to describe the object; provides a new set of coordinates that interpret how the image looks on a 2D plane. During a program's procedure, this calculation would need to occur between every frame. This allows the coordinates to incorporate changes to the object's scale and location within the 3D environment.

Below is an algorithm used to accomplish the projection of a 3D image. The algorithm performs the procedure of unpacking the polygons and modifying the contents of each vector.

```
polygons = [[-1,-1,1],[1,-1,1],[1,1,1],[-1,1,1],[-1,-1,-1],[1,-1,-1],[1,1,-1],[-1,1,-1]]
transformed_vertices = [0,1,2,3,4,5,6,7]

def rotate1(angle):
 for i in range (len(polygons)):
  a = polygons[i]
  b = [cos(angle), 0, sin(angle)]
  xpp = np.inner(a,b)
  b = [0, 1, 0]
```

```
    ypp = np.inner(a,b)
    b = [-sin(angle), 0, cos(angle)]
    zpp = np.inner(a,b)
    [xg[i], yg[i], zg[i]] = [xpp*scale+pos, ypp*scale+pos, zpp*scale+pos]

def drawPolygons():
edges = [[3,0],[3,7],[7,4],[4,0],[3,2],[7,6],[5,4],[1,0],[2,1],[1,5],[5,6],[6,2]]
    for edge in edges:
            pygame.draw.line(screen, black, transformed_vertices[edge[0]],
transformed_vertices[edge[1]], 5)

def project():
  for i in range(len(transformed_vertices)):
    # Perspective projection formula
    factor = xg[i]*.95/ (xg[i] + zg[i])
    xg[i] = xg[i] * factor
    factor = yg[i]/ (yg[i] + zg[i])
    yg[i] = yg[i] * factor
    x_screen = int(xg[i])
    y_screen = int(yg[i])
    transformed_vertices[i] = ((x_screen, y_screen))
    print(transformed_vertices)

while True:
    screen.fill((255,255,255))
    rotate1(angle)
    project()
    drawPolygons()
    angle += 0.01
```

The program contains several methods that creates the perception of a cube rotating in a 3D environment. As can be seen, the vector is rotated before being transformed into a projected 2D image. The methods used in this procedure are the same matrix calculations obtained in the previous chapters. These are rewritten into a series of multiplication functions, which take each coordinate in turn and returns the transformation or product of the calculation. The last stage of the program repopulates the vectors as a series of polygons. This is achieved by taking the vectors from the transformed_Vectors list containing the x and y coordinates.

TYPES OF 3D TO 2D PROJECTION	
PERSPECTIVE	Oblique Projection
ORTHOGRAPHIC PROJECTION	3-point projection
ISOMETRIC PROJECTION	Ariel projection
AXONOMETRIC PROJECTION:	Vanishing point

Table: 4.1.1 Mathematical processes used by the geometry shader

4.3.2 Projection within the Graphical Pipeline

The processes used within the 2D projection are achieved by repopulating the value of the vertices. The GPU completes this task along with rotation within the geometry shader. This allows the ALU to process the data before creating an expected image to pass the renderer. This set of coordinates represents any items held within 3D space. The renderer can then reformate the textures and colours to the final set of vertices. This last process happens separately from the geometry shader after the calculations have been completed on the data. This allows the GPU to coordinate the memory files that depict textures separately from the rest of the image.

The algorithm below identifies how the ALU functions during the procedure to complete the projection from a single 3D vector to a 2D coordinate.

```
section .data
   ; 3D point coordinates (X, Y, Z)
   X dd 2.0
   Y dd 3.0
   Z dd 4.0
   d dd 1.0 ; Focal length
   d_v dd 5.0 ; Viewer distance
   ; 2D point coordinates (x, y)
```

```
    x dd 0.0
    y dd 0.0

section .text
    global _start

_start:
    ; Load 3D coordinates into floating-point registers
    fld dword [X]
    fld dword [Y]
    fld dword [Z]
    ; Compute denominator (Z + d_v)
    fld dword [d_v]
    fadd st0, st1 ; st(0) = Z + d_v
    ; Compute x = (X * d) / (Z + d_v)
    fld dword [d] ; Load d
    fmul st0, st3 ; st(0) = X * d
    fdivp st1, st0 ; st(0) = (X * d) / (Z + d_v)
    fstp dword [x] ; Store x
    ; Compute y = (Y * d) / (Z + d_v)
    fld dword [d] ; Load d again
    fmul st0, st2 ; st(0) = Y * d
    fdivp st1, st0 ; st(0) = (Y * d) / (Z + d_v)
    fstp dword [y] ; Store y

    ; Exit the program
    mov eax, 1 ; syscall: exit
    xor ebx, ebx ; exit code 0
    int 0x80 ; interrupt to invoke syscall
```

Within 3D programming most forms of projection are created using perspective projection. This is a method of creating a 3D plane so that it closely mimics how the eye interprets the information found in the everyday world.

Summary of chapter

2D projection is one of the most important concepts to understand from a programming perspective. This concept underpins how the program creates a three-dimensional environment. Without considering the topic, it is not possible to create a 2D image that depicts how objects appear in the real world. 3D projection allows the program to simulate scale and render objects so that they contain both depth and perspective. The chapter has looked at the mathematics and programming that determine how this is accomplished.

End of Chapter Quiz

How is perspective projection used within 3D modelling?

List several ways that perspective can be achieved

How does distance affect the rendering of an object?

Describe how the geometry shader recalculates 2D projection.

CHAPTER 5

Camera movement and world coordinates

In this chapter, you will look at the following

- Setting up a camera and camera viewpoints
- Movement and rotation
- Using matrices for transformations
- Model view and worldview

5.1.1 Setting up a camera in a 3D environment

Within a 3D environment, the camera determines the current position and viewing angle for the images displayed. Due to the possibilities within a 3D engine, the camera can be positioned at any angle or height. This allows the perspective to be rotated or moved to follow specific points on the screen. Inside a 3D environment, the camera is seen as an object with its own specific location and coordinates. This allows the properties of the camera to be changed as needed, depending on the constraints of the program. This chapter is concerned with determining the rules that govern how a camera is created as an object and its properties. The chapter also looks at the worldview and homogenous coordinates as matrices to create a 2D projection.

5.1.2 The camera as an object

Due to the characteristics which determine 3D programming a camera is seen as an object with its own set of properties. This allows a program to update information used to position the camera and change any of the aspects that allow it to function. For instance, a camera will have a set of coordinates that determine the location and position across a set of axes. These can be updated each time the camera is expected to move. The camera object might also contain further sets of information, which can be changed depending on the intentions of the program. The purpose of this is to allow the program to adapt the use of the camera and also what part of the program it intends to describe.

At a basic level, the camera originally starts as a set of coordinates that describe the position and orientation as a series of vectors. For instance, a camera might be set at coordinates (0,0,0) with no rotation, pointing along the z-axis. The program will use these coordinates each time the camera moves or rotates. Updating the data used to describe the object.

PURPOSE OF CREATING A CAMERA OBJECT	
REPOSITIONING THE WORLD PERSPECTIVE	First-person gaming
SECONDARY CAMERAS	Cinematic viewing techniques
TRACKING	Saving camera coordinates
CLOSE-UP VIEWING POINT	Movement and rotation

Table: 5.1.2 How software uses camera tracking

5.1.3The viewing angle as a 2D plane

A program relies on the ability of the view to behave like an ordinary camera. The camera inside a program determines the properties used to create a 2D projection of the world's environment. Depending on the need of the software the camera can be either quite basic or have many advanced features. For the purpose of the chapter, it is only necessary to look at how the camera can move and rotate to change the current field of vision. This can be achieved at a basic level by simply moving the coordinates that are used to define the camera position. A projection matrix is then applied to convert the 3D vectors into a 2D plane. This topic has been looked at in previous chapters and uses the same set of calculations to achieve the final image.

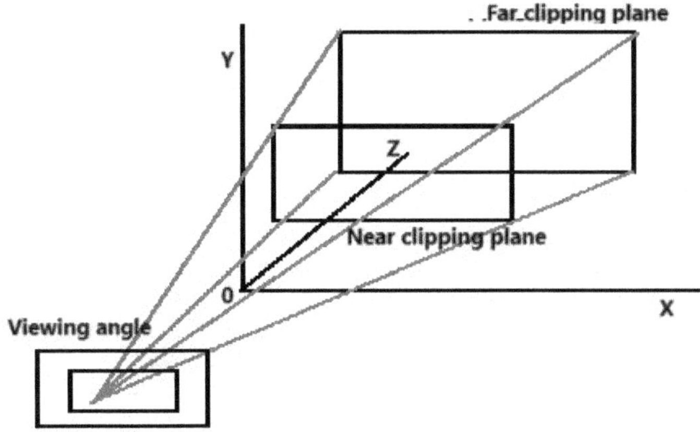

Fig: 5.1.3 The camera viewpoint as a projection

5.1.4 Camera movement and rotation

Most programs rely on a basic level of movement for the camera. This allows the camera to be repositioned and view objects from a different angle within space. In terms of movement, the camera behaves like any other object as it relies on the manipulation of the position of the vectors. The exception is that the camera coordinates also affect the calculation used to define the projection of the 2D image. For this reason, the camera might contain several other properties used to determine the characteristics of the 2D projection. During movement and rotation the camera can be repositioned by transforming the data held within the camera coordinates. This occurs through the racalculation of the vectors used to describe the objects location.

For example, a camera might need to be repositioned by moving the location 5 units along the x-axis, this would create a new set of coordinates to describe the camera position.

```
cameraNew (100,100,100)
newVector (5,0,0)
cameraNew (105,100,100)
```

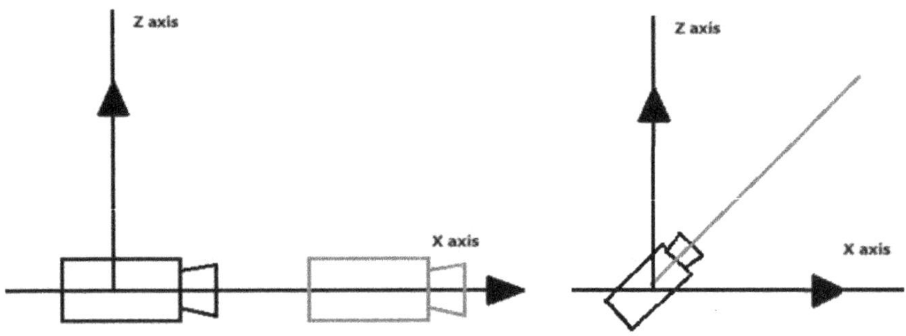

Fig: 5.1.3 Movement along the x-axis

The rotation occurs in a similar way where the calculation is held as a matrix used to change the world coordinates. Here an angle would be used to apply a transform to the current vector. During a single frame, the properties used to describe camera position and rotation are stored as a set of coordinates that are used to alter the dataset.

DIFFERENT CAMERA PROPERTIES	
POSITION	Viewing angle
ROTATION	Type of lens
ASPECT RATIO	Perspective
CLIPPING PLANES	blur

Table: 5.1.3 Summary of types of camera properties

5.2.1 The worldview as a coordinate system

A coordinate system allows a point to be identified within a three-dimensional area or space. The worldview within a 3D program is seen as a coordinate system using vectors to determine a direction along a given axis. A vector infers the distance of a point away from the original starting location. For most types of maps, this location will be seen as (0,0,0). The value within the vector will indicate the distance away from this point. This allows a point to be created within a single set of data and manipulated as necessary by the program. Here any points used to describe an object within the 3D space will all use the same coordinate system.

Here is an example of a three-dimensional point.

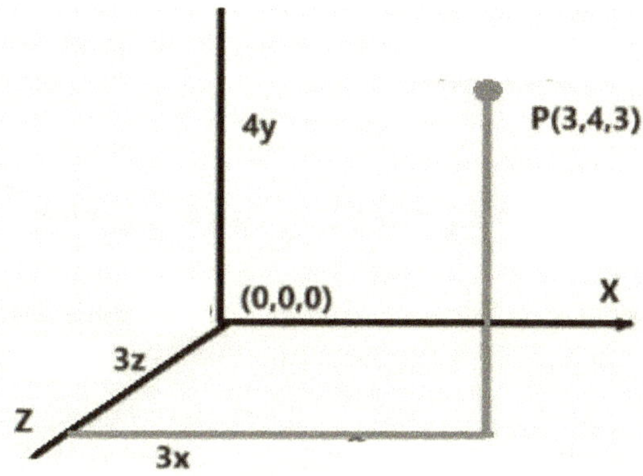

Fig: 5.2.1 a 3D coordinate system

During the camera transformation, the data held in the world coordinates are updated so that the starting position for the grid has moved places. This creates a sense of movement from the camera, as the objects appear as they are moving in one direction or another. The two diagrams explain how the camera movement affects the origin of the world coordinates.

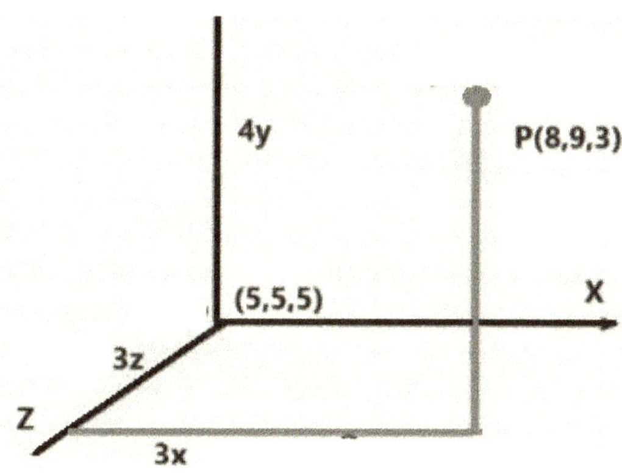

Fig: 5.2.1 A 3D coordinate system

As can be seen, the camera transform is used to reposition the starting point of the world coordinates. This process allows a new set of coordinates to be created that alters the location of any vectors held within the worldview. For instance, moving the camera along the x-axis would mean that the data held within the world matrix would also be updated. This is completed by transforming the worldview against a separate set of matrices used to describe movement, rotation and projection. The matrices infer how the camera transform alters the world coordinates.

5.2.2 Model view as opposed to the worldview

It is possible to update coordinates that determine the worldview to create a sense of movement within the camera. This alters the point at which an object is found inside a 3D environment. Determining object movement works similarly, but is coordinated within the model view or the specific coordinates used to create the object. These two coordinate systems are used within a program to determine whether the movement belongs either to the object or the 3D coordinates used to describe the area. Both systems use the same form of matrix transforms but refer to different sets of coordinate systems. For example, the model view will not interact with other objects.

5.2.3 The camera transform process

The process that occurs between the camera movement to the creation of a 2D image happens within a number of events. Here the processor has to coordinate any movements that occur before the image is cast onto a 2D plane. This includes changes in camera angle and also the rotation and movement of objects. To complete this process a series of matrices are used to store the information held for the world view as well as the transforms that then occur on screen. The process itself can be simplified into several stages such as:

Object position
World coordinates
Camera position
2D projection

$$\begin{bmatrix} X \\ Y \\ Z \\ 1 \end{bmatrix} \begin{bmatrix} r1, & r2, & r3, & t1 \\ r4, & r5, & r6, & t2 \\ r7, & r8, & r9, & t3 \end{bmatrix} \begin{bmatrix} fx, & 0, & cx \\ 0, & fx, & cy \\ 0, & 0, & 1 \end{bmatrix} = \begin{bmatrix} U \\ V \\ 1 \end{bmatrix}$$

3D world coordinates **Rotation and transformation** **Scalers** **2D Image coordinates**

Fig: 5.2.3 The Worldview transform

Here the original coordinates used to describe the objects held within the worldview, are notated as a single matrix. Before being recalculated depending on the information currently held within the transform. For instance, during a single frame, a camera might move three units and then rotate 90 degrees. This would mean that any object held within the world matrix would be simultaneously updated according to the information held in the transformation matrices.

This could be represented as the following

Vector	Translate	Rotate		Projection	2D image
[100]	[3]	[cos(90), sin(90)]	0,	[x/x+z]	[43.24]
[100]	[0]	[0, 1, 0]		[y/y+z]	[100]
[100]	[0]	[-sin(90), cos(90)]	0,	[0]	[0]

During a program, the coordinates used to describe the camera position might change continuously along with the position of the objects held within the world matrix. This process modifies any data simultaneously within the geometry shader, as the ALU updates the information regarding the world coordinates.

5.2.4 Matrices used within the camera transform

Transforming the information held within the world matrix involves the recalculation of each vector in turn. To simplify the process of creating the camera transform; each calculation can be rewritten as a set of matrices which can be updated as needed by the program. Here each calculation is written as a series of formulas that can redetermine the X, Y, or Z coordinate. A program might use several types of matrices transforms to recalculate the vectors, depending on the requirements of the program.

For example here are a few of the basic matrices that the camera transform might use during runtime.

Rotation matrix

Vector	Rotate X	Rotate Y	Rotate Z
[X]	[1,0,0]	[cos(angle), 0, sin(angle)]	[cos(angle0,- sin(angle,0]
[Y]	[0,cos(angle), - sin(angle)	[0, 1, 0]	Sin(angle),cos(angle),0]
[Z]	[0,sin(angle),cos(angle)	[-sin(angle), 0, cos(angle)]	[0,0,1]

Translation matrix

This matrix is used in a similar way to move world objects or the current position of the camera. The sum of the vectors is used to create the new transform.

Vector	translate		
[X]	[X+vector,	0,	0]
[Y]	[0,	Y+vectot,	0]
[Z]	[0,	0,	Z+vector]

Projection matrix

This matrix translates the three-point vector into a new 2D vector using just X and Y.

Vector	Projection		
[X]	[X/X+Z,	0,	0]
[Y]	[0,	Y/Y+Z	0]
[Z]	[0,	0,	0]

It is possible to use these single matrices to recalculate the position of coordinates within a program. The transforms are simply used as a reference point against functions that can redetermine the objects held in the worldview. It is also possible to use the matrices to reposition the camera and its rotation. Due to the camera being expected to complete other tasks during a program, it is possible to use other transforms that determine the quality or characteristics of the image.

5.2.5 Camera normalisation

Normalisation is the process of resetting the origin according to the movement of the camera, it occurs after the camera has moved and rotated. The purpose of normalisation is to correct the point of origin, so that the camera still rotates from the same position. At the end of the process the camera should be looking along the z axis away from the coordinates (0,0,0). How this occurs is by resetting the coordinates so that the camera sits at origin and the angle of direction is reset to 0.

The diagram below describes how this might appear within a set of detailed axes.

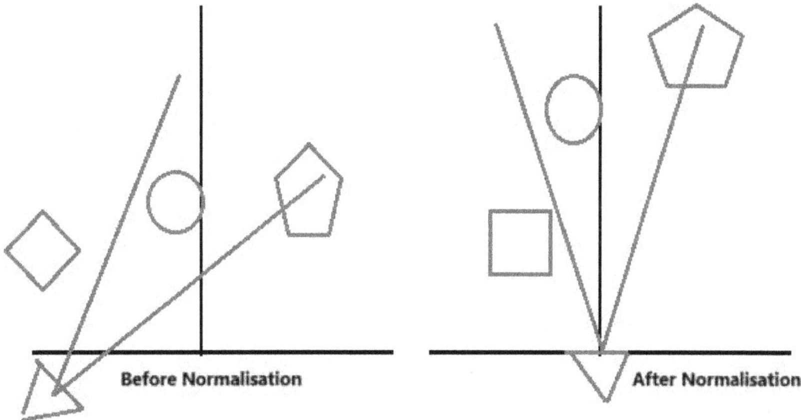

Fig:5.2.5 Determining the point of origin after repositioning the camera

The process of recalculating the origin can be written as a set of matrices which determines the new position of the origin from the last set of coordinates. This is effectively determining the distance covered between the last set of coordinates.

This can be represented in the following calculation.

```
Zaxis = normal(cameraPosition - cameraTarget)
Xaxis = normal(cross(cameraUpVector, Zaxis))
Yaxis = cross(Zaxis, Xaxis)
```

Without repositioning the origin, any further rotations will occur at the last point of the world view. Also the depth buffer will not be able to coordinate the position of objects along the z-axis. This procedure is important for determining the depth or range away from the camera during the rendering of objects by the fragment shader.

5.3.1 Using an algorithm for the camera movement

The final part of the chapter intends to provide an example of how an algorithm might be written so that a camera position can move and rotate, providing a new set of values within the worldview. Here a set of values titled world_coords are calculated by translating the vectors from the camera position and rotation matrix. This example describes how a set of matrices can be used to update the information held within the worldview.

```
import numpy as np

def camera_to_world(camera_coords, rotation_matrix, translation_
vector):
    Transforms camera coordinates to world coordinates.

Parameters:
    camera_coords (np.array): Coordinates in the camera view (3x1 vector).
    rotation_matrix (np.array): Rotation matrix (3x3 matrix).
    translation_vector (np.array): Translation vector (3x1 vector).

    Returns:
    np.array: Coordinates in the world view (3x1 vector).
    # Ensure inputs are numpy arrays
    camera_coords = np.array(camera_coords)
    rotation_matrix = np.array(rotation_matrix)
    translation_vector = np.array(translation_vector)
```

```
    # Transform the coordinates
    world_coords = np.dot(rotation_matrix.T, (camera_coords - ranslation_
vector))

    return world_coords

# Example usage
camera_coords = np.array([1, 2, 3])
rotation_matrix = np.array([[0.866, -0.5, 0],
                            [0.5, 0.866, 0],
                            [0, 0, 1]])
translation_vector = np.array([1, 1, 1])

world_coords = camera_to_world(camera_coords, rotation_matrix,
translation_vector)
print("World Coordinates:", world_coords)
```

Summary of chapter

This chapter has described the conventions used to create a camera within a 3D environment. A camera has its own set of properties that can be updated to change the dimensions to produce a 2D projection. Homogenous coordinates were also looked at, as camera movement relies on recalculating sets of three-dimensional vectors. For this purpose matrices are used to create the calculations for large sets of data.

End of Chapter Quiz

Why are matrices used to calculate vector data types?

Other than perspective list three types of camera properties

Describe the stages used for camera projection.

What is the purpose of defining the clipping planes?

CHAPTER 6

Textures and rendering

In this chapter, you will look at the following

- Colour rendering
- Z depth buffer and rendering the foreground
- The fragment shader
- Texture and texture layers

6.1.1 The rendering process

The geometry shader in the graphics pipeline is responsible for producing the 2D projected coordinates from a series of 3D vectors. The second part of the pipeline adds colour and textures to the final image. This is completed in several ways dependent on the type of processes chosen to complete the task. At a basic level, a 3D image can be simply rendered as several shapes used to separate the objects. More complicated processes use a fragment shader or a texture map, to provide a more realistic and detailed finish. This chapter aims to define how this process is achieved and the types of methods that are available to complete the rendering of a 3D environment.

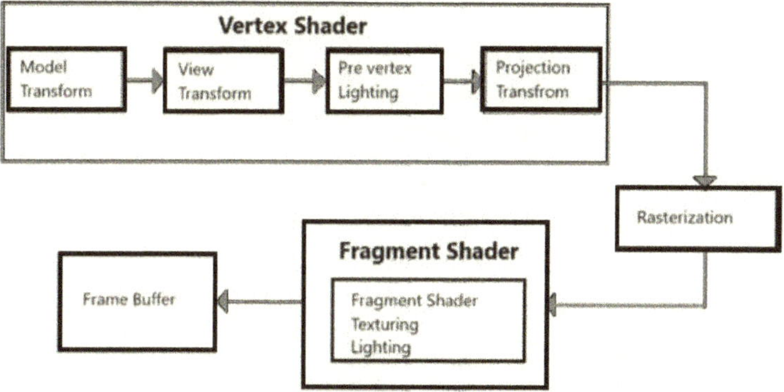

Fig: 6.1.1 The fragment shader in the graphics pipeline

6.1.2 Rendering an object and adding colour

At a basic level rendering the objects that exist within the 3D space is completed by allowing the polygons to be drawn as a simple algorithm. After passing the geometry shader, each set of polygons will have an X and Y coordinate that has been recalculated to include the projection onto the 2D plane. These new vectors can be used to draw each polygon onto the screen as a simple set of shapes. This allows for a simple procedure to render and colour the 3D models.

The program below is an example of how a program can determine the position of a set of polygons on the screen

```
# Vertices of the cube
vertices = [[-1, -1, -1],[1, -1, -1],[1, 1, -1], [-1, 1, -1],
   [-1, -1, 1],[1, -1, 1],[1, 1, 1],[-1, 1, 1]]

# Faces of the cube (each face is a list of 4 vertex indices)
faces = [
   (0, 1, 2, 3), (4, 5, 6, 7), (0, 1, 5, 4),
   (2, 3, 7, 6), (1, 2, 6, 5), (4, 7, 3, 0)]

# Function to project 3D points to 2D
def project_point(point, scale=100, offset=(width//2, height//2)):
   x = int(point[0] * scale + offset[0])
   y = int(-point[1] * scale + offset[1])
   return x, y

# Function to draw faces with colors
def draw_faces(faces, vertices, colors):
   for index, face in enumerate(faces):
      face_vertices = [vertices[i] for i in face]
            pygame.draw.polygon(screen, colors[index % len(colors)],
[project_point(v) for v in face_vertices])
```

The algorithm takes the coordinates that determine the points of the polygon and draws them as a series of 2D shapes. Each of the points that define the polygon will have been passed through the geometry shader.

Meaning that the image should include the camera movement and change in depth of the 3D projection. Due to the simplicity of the algorithm, the output only defines the shape at a basic level and will not show shadow or determine the start or end of an object's shape.

This might be depicted as the following.

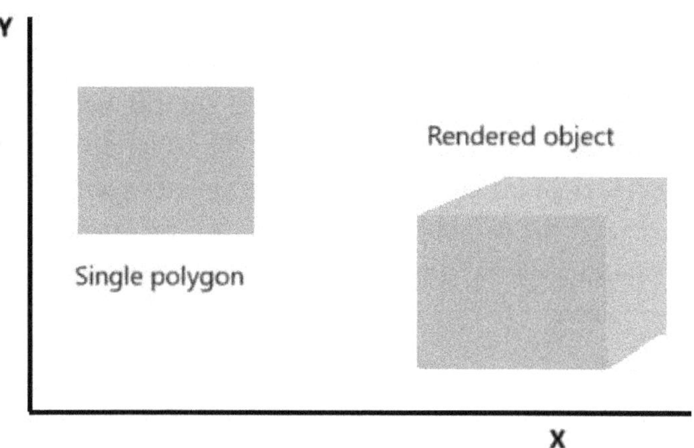

Fig 6.1.2 Using polygons to shade objects

The above diagram details a single polygon being rendered as a separate shape. The object next to it is a set of polygons used to define an object. During the rendering process, an object or model will be created by rendering each polygon according to the information found within the geometry shader. This part of the process completed by the fragment shader will also add light and texture to the image.

ROLE OF THE FRAGMENT SHADER	
PIXEL COLOURING	Special effects
TEXTURING	Post-processing
LIGHT AND SHADOW	Colour correction
ALPHA COLOURING	Depth testing

Table: 6.1.2 The fragment shader within the graphics pipeline

6.2.1 The Z-buffer and creating perspective

Designing an image in 3D involves several aspects that allow the image to be perceived with a sense of perspective. One of the purposes of the geometry shader is to create a camera image that allows for depth once it has been projected onto a 2D plane. Another way that perspective is achieved within the GPU is the placing of objects in front of each other, dependent on where the objects appear in terms of relation to the camera. To achieve this the Z-axis is used to determine the distance that an object is from the background. The Z axis is part of the vector that indicates how far an object is from the centre of the viewing point or origin.

For instance, the two objects pictured below are framed within two separate z coordinates that determine which object appears first within the view of the camera.

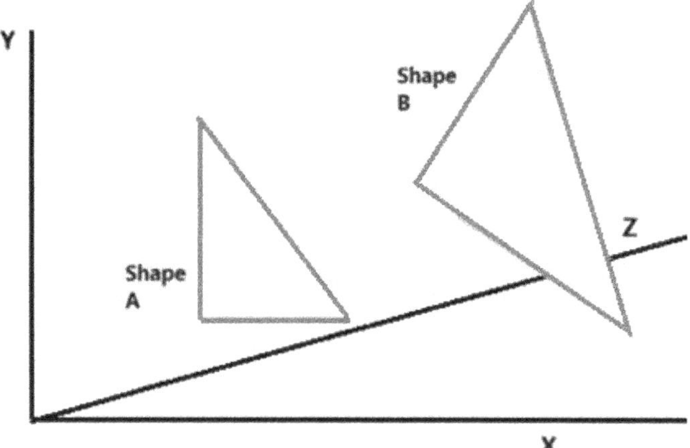

Fig 6.2.1 A set of shapes at different points along the z-axis

When the image above is redrawn using the camera viewpoint; shape A should be redrawn in front of shape B. This would create the perception of a 3D perspective, as the camera perceives the objects closest to the camera first.

6.2.2 An algorithm to determine the Z-axis

For the GPU to determine the range in which an object appears, the processor determines the Z value for each of the points used to draw the object's shape. By establishing the z value held for each point within the vectors it is possible to process images in an order that allows the camera to differentiate the range of the object.

The program below is written in ASM. It details how the z value is found by using a set of registers to hold each vector in turn.

```
; Input: Pixel position and depth
; Output: Color if pixel is in foreground, discard otherwise

; Pseudocode for fragment shader
main:
   ; Load pixel position
   MOV R0, pixel_position
   ; Load depth value of current pixel
   MOV R1, depth_value

   ; Load depth buffer value at pixel position
   TEX R2, R0, depth_buffer
   ; Compare current pixel depth with depth buffer value
   CMP R3, R1, R2 ; R3 = (R1 < R2) ? 1 : 0

   ; If R3 is 1, the current pixel is in the foreground
   IF R3 == 1:
      ; Output the color of the pixel (foreground color)
      MOV output_color, foreground_color
   ELSE:
      ; Discard the pixel (background)
      DISCARD

   ; End of shader program
   END
```

What occurs in the program, is that the vectors used for the current frame are passed into the depth buffer. These are then moved into the four registers, before determining which value is in the foreground of the rendered picture. This allows the correct pixel to appear within the contexts of the outputted image. The procedure explores how the polygons drawn onto the screen can be defined within a sense of perspective. Within a program, this procedure might be completed each time an object or a polygon intends to be drawn onto the screen. The depth buffer is used to determine the order in which elements of the picture appear within the frame.

6.3.1 Colouring inside the fragment shader

The fragment shader is a part of the shader that determines how the objects are coloured and creates the final render of the geometric model on the screen. The shader works alongside the z_buffer to colour the polygons according to the distance a point is along the z-axis. For instance, a polygon might have three points all with the colour (255,127,0). When a point is drawn onto the screen by the fragment shader, the colour will be determined by the value held within the z_buffer. This simple effect allows an image to be shaded according to where they are positioned from the camera. The following image represents how a fragment shader might determine the shade of a rendered shape.

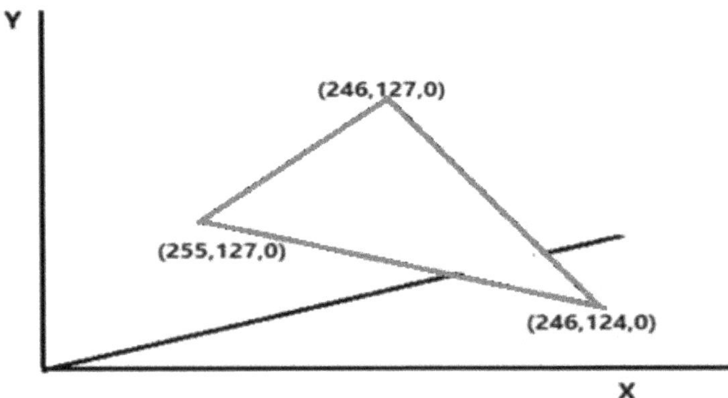

Fig:6.3.1 Defining a set of points within the polygon shader

Here the polygon is drawn from the values used to describe each vector. The fragment shader then determines the density of the colour dependent on the value of the Z-buffer. This gives the effect of shadow or depth. The same effect can be done with multiple colours except the points have to be identified by the fragment shader to determine each of the RGB colour ranges.

For example here is a polygon with separate colours used for each point according to the index mapped onto the vector.

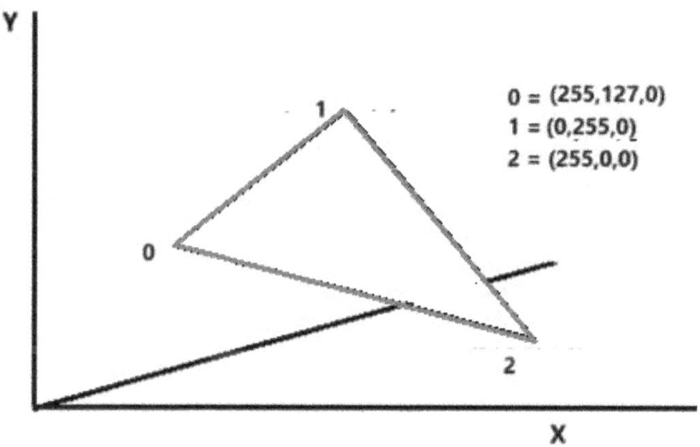

Fig: 6.3.1 Mapping the points within the fragment shader.

As can be seen from the picture, the points within a polygon can be mapped to pre-existing colour ranges. When the polygon passes through the shader, each point is rendered according to the colour found within the index. Here the separate points are given an identity and a reference to the colour map. The fragment shader is then able to determine how the polygon is rendered before being drawn onto the screen.

For example
Point1 vector = (250,150,200)
Point1 Index = (0,1,2)
Point1 RGB = (255,127,0),(0,255,0),(255,0,0)

HOW THE FRAGMENT SHADER CREATES PERSPECTIVE	
DEPTH CALCULATION	Shadows and Highlights
DEPTH BUFFERING	Texture Mapping
PERSPECTIVE CORRECT INTERPOLATION	Colour and Material Effects
LIGHTING MODELS	Post-Processing Effects

Table: 6.3.1 Perspective within the fragment shader

6.4.1 Texture mapping and high-density textures

Part of the process of the fragment shader is to apply textures to polygons dependent on the intentions of the program. This is coordinated by applying textures saved in the memory cache of the GPU and stretching these onto the shape of the polygon. A polygon does not retain a single shape throughout a program. Instead, the texture has to be mapped so that the image can be applied to the points referring to the polygon outline.

The image below identifies how to map the points onto a shape.

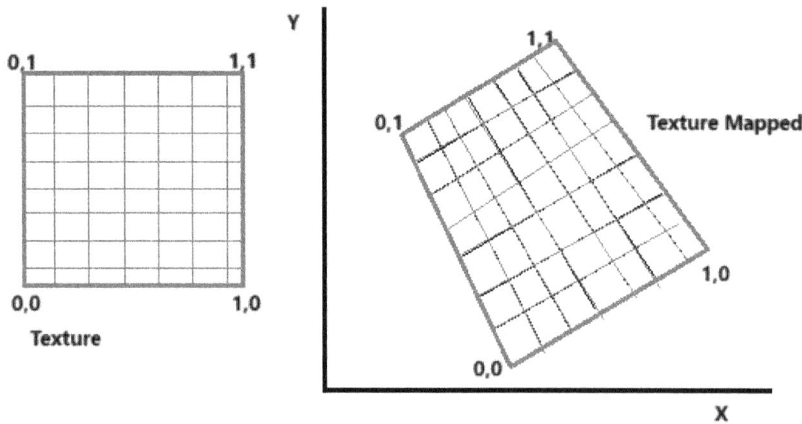

Fig:6.4.1 Mapping a texture to a polygon

The process of mapping the shape can be completed by binding the texture to an object or set of polygons. This occurs as a similar process to mapping a shader, except the program has to stretch the image onto the moving outline of the shape. This is achieved by iterating a set of pixels onto the mapped points, during each frame. As this is work intensive for the computer processor. This type of program often relies on the memory of the GPU to complete the task.

An example of a function to apply a texture is written below.

```
# Texture coordinates
tex_coords = [(0, 0), (1, 0),
  (1, 1), (0, 1)]

# Function to project 3D points to 2D
def project_point(point, scale=300, offset=(width//2, height//2)):
  x = int(point[0] * scale + offset[0])
  y = int(-point[1] * scale + offset[1])
  return x, y

# Function to draw textured faces
def draw_textured_faces(faces, vertices, tex_coords, texture):
  for face in faces:
    face_vertices = [vertices[i] for i in face]
    points_2d = [project_point(v) for v in face_vertices]
    # Create a surface for the face
    face_surface = pygame.Surface((256, 256))
    face_surface.blit(texture, (0, 0))

    # Map the texture onto the face
    tex_points = [(tc[0] * 256, tc[1] * 256) for tc in tex_coords]
    pygame.draw.polygon(screen, black, points_2d, 0)
    pygame.transform.scale(face_surface, (points_2d[2][0] - points_
2d[0][0], points_2d[2][1] - points_2d[0][1]))
    pygame.gfxdraw.textured_polygon(screen, points_2d, face_surface,
0, 0)
```

As can be seen, the image for the texture is scaled into a relevant set of pixel parameters for the polygon. This is then stretched onto the map of the shape by iterating between each point within the polygon, with a set of pixels derived from the texture image.

6.4.2 High-density textures

High-density textures are a popular method of creating reflection and shadow within an image. These work in a similar way to normal texture maps. Except a texture will contain several layers used for the image. The rest will contain information on the refraction of light and shadow. High-density texture maps are mainly used to create more detail within a 3D environment; and add effects to objects that cast shadow and reflection such as metallic substances, fluid, or particles.

TYPES OF TEXTURE MAP	
ALBEDO	Specular
NORMAL	Opacity
ROUGHNESS	Ambient occlusion
METALNESS	Specular

Table: 6.4.2 Types of texture effects

There are a number of types of maps that can be applied to a texture effecting how the material appears within an environment. For instance a map that effects the objects normal increases the way that light reacts to indentations within the image. While specular maps are used to change the way light reflects form the given material. By using texture maps within a scene it is possible to increase the level of detail used to render an image.

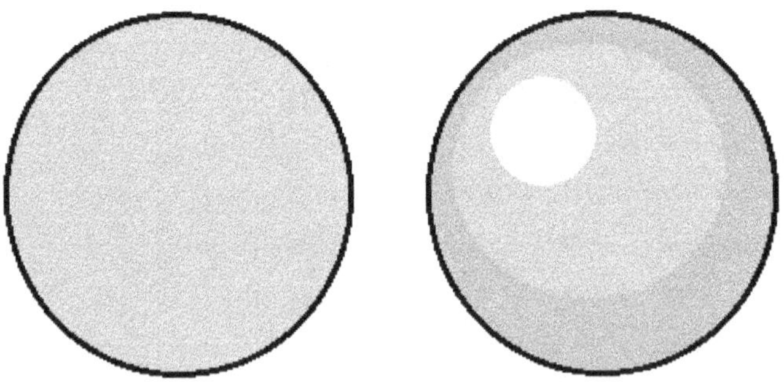

Fig 6.4.2 adding specular lighting to a texture

Summary of chapter

The fragment shader is the last stage of the graphics pipeline and includes the rendering of the objects as well as any light and shadow effects. The chapter has explored how the geometric data is rendered to create the colour and texture of the objects. The chapter also explored some of the techniques used to render the objects. Such as the relevance of the Z-buffer to determine the order in which the polygons are drawn onto the foreground.

End of Chapter Quiz

What techniques are used to establish a 3D environment?

How does the fragment shader differ from the rest of the graphics pipeline

List several purposes of the fragment shader.

Describe how a texture might be mapped to a set of points.

CHAPTER 7

Light and shadow

In this chapter, you will look at the following

- Types of lighting effects
- Shadow
- Texture mapping and real-time lighting
- Ray-casting

7.1.1 Processing a light effect in the fragment shader

Light and shadow is another process completed by the fragment shader within the graphics pipeline; and can provide more detail to a 3D environment. There are several ways to implement lighting as an effect, depending on the type of light and the process that is required. For instance, a light map is an easy way to add a lighting source to an image, whereas real-time shaders require the processor to complete many computations during runtime. To provide a lighting source in many modern forms of software, the GPU has a series of ray-caster processors that can determine the direction of point lighting and how reflection affects the objects within an environment.

7.1.2 Directional lighting vs area.

The type of lighting depends on the source in which the light is emitted and the effect that the light intends to create. For example, a lighting source could be created using a directional spotlight, or an ambient type of lighting source, such as a skybox. This determines the range of the lit area and the angle that is cast by the shadow. For example, the directional lighting effect has a narrow range but a more intense shadow. There are also other types of lighting sources such as area lights that can illuminate a broader area within a program but only cast a diffuse shadow. The program to run a lighting effect depends on the type of procedure chosen and also the intention of the lighting properties.

Here is an example diagram to indicate the difference between directional lighting and an area light.

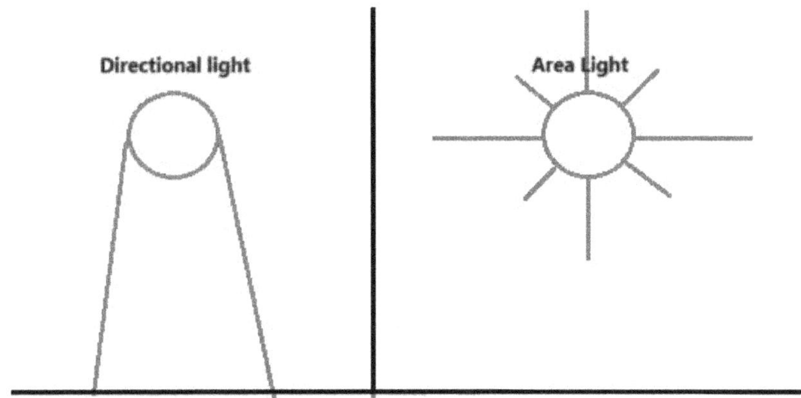

Fig: 7.1.2 Directional and area light

The next picture determines examples of a shadow being cast by an object.

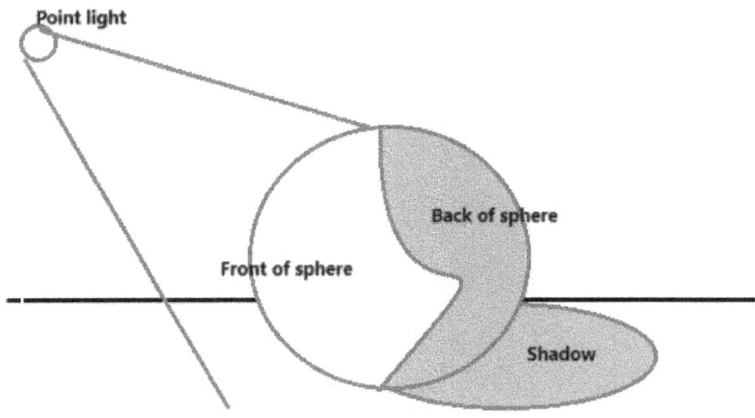

Fig: 7.1.2 Directional and area lighting

It is possible to see that the shadow being cast is determined by the type of lighting effect and the luminance or intensity of the source. For instance, area lights diffuse more within the environment, meaning that the shadow cast reflects less of the object's shape while it is being drawn.

7.1.3 Ambient Lighting vs Specular

Both types of light sources can be used interchangeably depending on the needs of the program, and provide two separate methods of lighting an area. Specular lighting creates more reflection and a stronger shadow that can be seen to affect the object. Diffuse lighting works well for area lights, as this is more ambient and does not cast shadows on the surrounding objects. Due to the effect specular lighting can achieve with a directional light source, this is more popular when considering the cinematic effects within a scene. Again the program to create these types of effects relies on how well the processor can run the tasks. Rendering scenes that are lit from several sources can put a demand on the schedules being completed by the GPU.

TYPES OF LIGHTING AN EFFECT	
DIRECTIONAL	Diffuse
AREA LIGHTING	Ambient
SPOTLIGHT	Specular
POINT LIGHTING	Emissive

Table: 7.3.1 Perspective within the fragment shader

7.2.1 Texture Maps to create a lighting effect

Due to the complexity of adding multiple light sources to a 3D environment. Using a light map is a simple method of adding light without needing the GPU to process large amounts of data. Light maps are an effective solution for creating light sources that are not affected by other processes occurring at the same time. A light map works by altering the texture of a stationary polygon before the polygon is drawn into the 3D space. This allows the area to look like there are a series of light sources available as the textures have been recoloured to produce the existence of light. There are several methods of creating a light map such as baking the map or simply drawing each of the textures used to create the polygon. This procedure is completed before runtime and puts less demand on the processor than other types of lighting effects.

The process of creating a light map is determined by placing the lights onto the map or area of the 3D space and projecting a light source onto the given textures. A procedure known as baking the light map allows the textures to be redrawn on separate software, to infer the locations where the light had affected the intended texture.

Below is an example of altering the texture according to the information presented from the application of UV light.

IMAGE 32

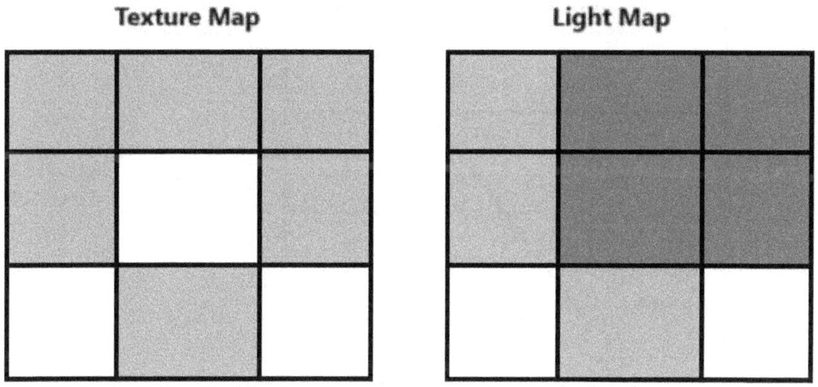

Texture Map **Light Map**

As can be seen, the new texture is identical in shape to the first. Although the new light map allows a small amount of shadow to be detected within the coordination of pixels.

7.3.1 Creating light through ray-casting

Ray-casting is a technique to determine what elements within a frame are held within a light source. Using this technique it is possible to determine shadow and create several different types of effects by applying a light source to a scene. Due to the importance of using ray-casting to create lighting and reflection. Modern GPUs are designed with several ray-caster modules per core. These modules work by determining the position a light beam would strike an object. Once determined the object's colour or part of it will be redrawn to apply the effect of the light source. Once a light source has been set up using this method it is possible to cast any number of light rays until the scene has been effectively rendered. Again it is necessary to mention that the processor struggles to create this effect per frame without the use of the GPU.

The diagram below looks at the calculation to determine the distance and position of a beam of light. For instance, a position is given for the light and angle of view that it covers. The ray-caster will then continue to rework this calculation across the entire field of view. During the rendering process, the calculations determine the light's effect across a single frame.

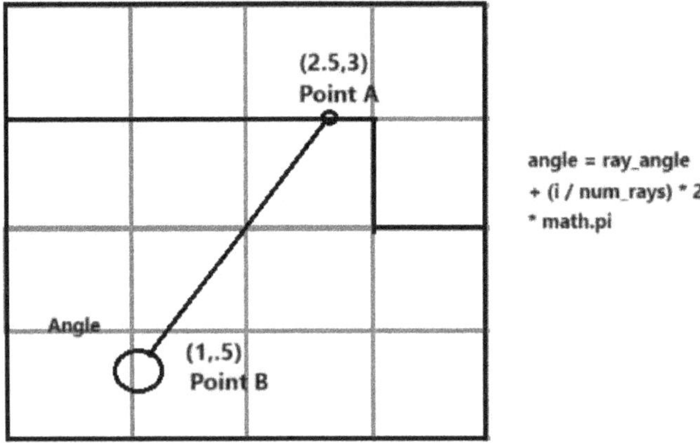

Fig 7.3.1 Determining a point of refraction

As can be see the source of the light is given as point A and an intersection point B determines when the light source has struck an object or element from within the scene. This process is required to continue across the frame to render the whole scene.

7.3.2 Program to simulate ray-casting

To further explain the process that the processor completes to render the scene's lighting. The procedure has been written into a program that draws a line of light from the centre of the screen. Increasing the angle of sight for each iteration.

```
# Ray properties
ray_angle = 0
num_rays = 100
ray_length = 300

# Cube properties
cube_center = (WIDTH // 2, HEIGHT // 2)
cube_size = 100

# Main loop
    # Clear screen
    screen.fill(BLACK)

    # Draw cube
    pygame.draw.rect(screen, WHITE, (cube_center[0] - cube_size // 2,
cube_center[1] - cube_size // 2, cube_size, cube_size), 2)

    # Draw rays
    for i in range(num_rays):
        angle = ray_angle + (i / num_rays) * 2 * math.pi
        end_x = cube_center[0] + ray_length * math.cos(angle)
        end_y = cube_center[1] + ray_length * math.sin(angle)
        pygame.draw.line(screen, WHITE, cube_center, (end_x, end_y), 1)

    # Update display
    pygame.display.flip()

    # Rotate rays
    ray_angle += 0.01
```

The program demonstrates the types of procedures the processor needs to complete to calculate the refraction of light at point B. During a program, any elements that are within the location of point B will be redrawn by the shader to reflect the adaptation to the light source.

Summary of chapter

Lighting within a scene can add more detail and improve the level of realism. This chapter has tried to describe the type of ways in which lighting can be achieved within a program, as well as common types of effects used. For instance, lighting maps are a less complicated way of achieving a sense of lighting. In contrast, using complex ray casters can determine the effects of shadow and reflection of complex materials such as water.

End of Chapter Quiz

List several types of lighting effects

Why are texture maps less demanding for the processor?

Describe reflection works on high-density textures.

What are point lights and how do they interact with the environment?

PART 2

Programming and hardware concepts

CHAPTER 8

Programming the GPU and OpenGL

In this chapter, you will look at the following

- The OpenGL library
- Basic concepts
- Binding materials
- Using Normal's for lighting

6.1.1 What is OpenGL

OpenGL is a library that is able to use the added functionality of the GPU. Using the OpenGL extension indicates that the graphics processor is being called by the methods used within the statements. Due to the graphics card calling procedures differently from the CPU, OpenGL needs more contexts to run a basic routine. The reason is that the program often has to bind materials to vectors or clear the graphics buffer between frames. This makes programming the GPU more complicated but allows for the processor to handle more tasks and improve the functionality of the programs. OpenGL is an extention library called at the beginning of the program to allow the routine statements to be called during runtime.

6.1.2 Adding OpenGL as an extension

Running OpenGL is completed by adding the extension to the script editor used to run the programs. For example the below extension is added to Python. Allowing the methods written inside the library to be used within the program.

```
import pygame
from pygame.locals import *
```

```
from OpenGL.GL import *
from OpenGL.GLU import *

from Cube import *
from LoadMesh import *
```

This adds the functionality of OpenGL to the program and allows the program to call procedures that use the GPU to run.

ADVANTAGES OF USING OPENGL TO RUN PROGRAMS	
PARALLEL PROCESSING	Energy Efficiency
SPEED	Improved Performance
MACHINE LEARNING & AI	High Memory Bandwidth
GRAPHICS RENDERING:	Versatility

Table: 6.3.1 Perspective within the fragment shader

6.1.3 Calling a statement in OpenGL

The library is written in a set of parentheses that indicates that each method belongs to the OpenGL extension. For example a routine might depend on a function written within OpenGL and be called to complete a task. The method itself calls the procedure written inside the extension.

For example, a basic statement might be used to call a window for the program.

```
if not glfw.init():
    raise Exception("GLFW can't be initialized")

# Create a windowed mode window and its OpenGL context
window = glfw.create_window(640, 480, "New Window GL", None,
None)
if not window:
    glfw.terminate()
    raise Exception("GLFW window can't be created")
```

As can be seen the process for creating the statement is similar to any other procedure. Except the methods called have the prefix GL. Indicating that the statement uses the OpenGL interface.

8.2.1 Setting up Vertices in OpenGL

The procedure for creating an object within OpenGL is slightly different from running the same procedure on the CPU. The reason is that the information containing the vectors for the model needs to be stored within the GPU's memory cache. The program then loads the file as its object and can access and change the coordinates as requested during runtime.

Here is an example of how a mesh can be added to a program as a separate folder or file.

```
def load_mesh(file_path):
    vertices = []
    faces = []

    with open(file_path, 'r') as file:
        for line in file:
            if line.startswith('v '): # Vertex
                vertex = list(map(float, line.strip().split()[1:]))
                vertices.append(vertex)
            elif line.startswith('f '): # Face
                face = list(map(int, line.strip().split()[1:]))
                faces.append(face)

    return vertices, faces

def draw_mesh(vertices, faces):
    glBegin(GL_TRIANGLES)
    for face in faces:
        for vertex in face:
            glVertex3fv(vertices[vertex - 1])
    glEnd()
```

As can be seen, OpenGL has its own method for loading the vectors. Usually, the CPU would hold the coordinates as a list and change the data by accessing existing indexes for the vector's coordinates. The procedure within OpenGL uses the memory inside the GPU to store the coordinates. This allows for larger data sets to be accessed by the GPU simultaneously. The GPU has a set of registers to change the information contained within the mesh. This procedure highlights the use of the processor inside OpenGL, as the connotation to create the program requires a different set of routines to complete the task.

8.2.2 Rotation and translation of an object

The principle used to create movement for an object within OpenGL relies upon the transformation of the values within the vector coordinates. The difference with the GPU is that altering the coordinates is achieved simultaneously inside the memory. For this reason, the program needs to push the matrices into the memory of the GPU, before altering the coordinates. The translation and rotation of the object are achieved by altering the values held for the vertices to reposition them inside the worldview. The function alters the values according to the new position of the object.

Here is an example of transforming the object within the worldview.

```
pygame.display.set_mode(display, DOUBLEBUF | OPENGL)
gluPerspective(45, (display[0] / display[1]), 0.1, 50.0)
glTranslatef(0.0, 0.0, -5)

translation = [0.0, 0.0, 0.0]
rotation_angle = 0

while True:
        translation[0] -= 0.1
        translation[1] += 0.1
        rotation_angle -= 5
```

```
glClear(GL_COLOR_BUFFER_BIT | GL_DEPTH_BUFFER_BIT)
glPushMatrix()
glTranslatef(*translation)
glRotatef(rotation_angle, 0, 1, 0)
draw_mesh(vertices, faces)
```

As can be seen, the program works the same way as the processor, except the caches holding the value for the depth coordinates need to be cleared between each frame. This allows a new set of values to be loaded for the next routine.

8.2.3 Setting up a camera

To determine the position of the camera within OpenGL, the matrices used to calculate the transforms are written as a series of uniforms. These are simply a set of matrix coordinates that cannot be altered within the space of the program. For instance, the projection and view matrix used within the camera transform are written as a set of uniform calculations. These allow the program to refer back to the matrix wherever the program requires this calculation to be performed, reducing the need for code. The values entered into the uniforms are written on a separate header file that is linked to the program. These can be called at any time to perform the procedure. The program uses the transforms to create the correct position of the objects on screen, translating the image coordinates before projecting them as a 2D image.

The program below demonstrates how calling the procedure is completed in OpenGL.

```
# Camera settings
camera_pos = glm.vec3(0.0, 0.0, 3.0)
camera_target = glm.vec3(0.0, 0.0, 0.0)
camera_direction = glm.normalize(camera_pos - camera_target)
camera_right = glm.normalize(glm.cross(glm.vec3(0.0, 1.0, 0.0), camera_
direction))
camera_up = glm.cross(camera_direction, camera_right)
```

```
# Set up the view, projection, and model matrices
view = glm.lookAt(camera_pos, camera_target, camera_up)
projection = glm.perspective(glm.radians(45.0), 800 / 600, 0.1, 100.0)
model = glm.mat4(1.0)

# Pass the matrices to the shader program
model_loc = glGetUniformLocation(shader_program, "model")
view_loc = glGetUniformLocation(shader_program, "view")
projection_loc = glGetUniformLocation(shader_program, "projection")
glUniformMatrix4fv(model_loc, 1, GL_FALSE, glm.value_ptr(model))
glUniformMatrix4fv(view_loc, 1, GL_FALSE, glm.value_ptr(view))
glUniformMatrix4fv(projection_loc, 1, GL_FALSE, glm.value_
ptr(projection))
```

As can be seen, the procedure to call the function ascertains the position and rotation of the camera before normalizing the origin to match the position along the z-axis. The uniform matrices are required to perform the calculations for elements of the camera positions that update the model and view coordinates. As well as changing the projection of the 2D image.

8.2.4 The Fragment shader

The purpose of the fragment shader is to add colour and light to a rendered polygon. By ascertaining the position of a shape according to the information stored within the Z_buffer, the fragment shader can adjust the colour ratio at a given vector. This type of shading can be used to provide the appearance of depth to an object, and the effects of adding a light source to a scene.

Below is a program that applies a shader to a set of objects.

```
def create_shader_program(vertex_source, fragment_source):
 vertex_shader = compile_shader(vertex_source, GL_VERTEX_
SHADER)
 fragment_shader = compile_shader(fragment_source, GL_
FRAGMENT_SHADER)
```

```
    # Create shader program and link shaders
    program = glCreateProgram()
    glAttachShader(program, vertex_shader)
    glAttachShader(program, fragment_shader)
    glLinkProgram(program)

    # Check for linking errors
    if not glGetProgramiv(program, GL_LINK_STATUS):
        error = glGetProgramInfoLog(program)
        raise Exception(f"Program linking failed: {error.decode()}")

    # Clean up shaders (they're no longer needed after linking)
    glDeleteShader(vertex_shader)
    glDeleteShader(fragment_shader)
    return program

# Set up the triangle vertices
vertices = np.array([
    0.0, 0.5, 0.0,
    -0.5, -0.5, -1.0,
    0.5, -0.5, 0.0,], dtype=np.float32)

# Create vertex buffer object (VBO) and vertex array object (VAO)
VBO = glGenBuffers(1)
VAO = glGenVertexArrays(1)

# Bind VAO and VBO
glBindVertexArray(VAO)
glBindBuffer(GL_ARRAY_BUFFER, VBO)
glBufferData(GL_ARRAY_BUFFER, vertices.nbytes, vertices, GL_
STATIC_DRAW)

# Define vertex data layout
glVertexAttribPointer(0, 3, GL_FLOAT, GL_FALSE, 3 * vertices.
itemsize, ctypes.c_void_p(0))
glEnableVertexAttribArray(0)
```

```
# Unbind VAO and VBO
glBindBuffer(GL_ARRAY_BUFFER, 0)
glBindVertexArray(0)

# Create and use the shader program
shader_program = create_shader_program(vertex_shader_source,
fragment_shader_source)
glUseProgram(shader_program)
```

As can be seen, the procedure for implementing the fragment shader involves several processes. First, the shader that is being used needs to be referenced. As this is dependent on the purpose of the intended program. The shader is then bound to the object so that the GPU can determine what object belongs to each shader. The processor is then able to infer how the shader will render the particular object.

8.2.5 Adding texture to a shape

Binding a texture to an object is similar to adding a fragment shader. The texture itself is simply added to the shape by binding the image, the GPU is then able to complete the process of positioning the texture onto the object's vertices. This allows the texture to appear on the object once it is rendered.

Here is an example of binding an image to a single shape.

```
def load_texture(path):
    image = Image.open("imgs/texture.jpg")
    image = image.transpose(Image.FLIP_TOP_BOTTOM)
    img_data = np.array(image, dtype=np.uint8)

    texture = glGenTextures(1)
    glBindTexture(GL_TEXTURE_2D, texture)

        glTexImage2D(GL_TEXTURE_2D, 0, GL_RGB, image.width,
image.height, 0, GL_RGB, GL_UNSIGNED_BYTE, img_data)
    glGenerateMipmap(GL_TEXTURE_2D)
    return texture
```

The GPU binds the image to the object and can add new dimensions to the shape once the object is repositioned or moved. According to the behaviour of the program.

TASKS OPENGL SHARES WITH THE CPU	
RENDERING	Clipping
SHADING	Lighting
TEXTURE MAPPING	Depth Testing
TRANSFORMATION	Anti-Aliasing

Table: 6.3.1 How OpenGL shares tasks with CPU

8.3.1 Creating a Light Source

The fragment shader is responsible for adding depth and colour to the objects created in OpenGL. It is also possible to use the shader to add lighting effects to the rendered objects within a program. This occurs because the shader created reacts to different points within the 3D environment to provide the effect of light being transmitted across the different sources. During the program, the shader will react to the light source by altering the colour of the vertex's points. Simulating the effect of lighting within a scene.

Here is an example of a shader used to alter the colour used to shade an object.

```
# Fragment Shader
FRAGMENT_SHADER = """
#version 330
uniform vec2 u_resolution;
uniform vec2 u_lightPos;
uniform float u_time;
out vec4 fragColor;
void main() {
   vec2 uv = gl_FragCoord.xy / u_resolution;
   vec2 lightDir = u_lightPos - gl_FragCoord.xy;
```

```
float dist = length(lightDir);
float intensity = 1.0 / (dist * dist);
vec3 color = vec3(intensity * sin(u_time), intensity * cos(u_time), intensity);
fragColor = vec4(color, 1.0);}"""
```

Another method of creating a light source is to use Normal's to position the light and use the procedure within the GPU to shade the object. Using a normal is simply a method of determining the direction of the light to a particular point, by obtaining the angle of the point's axis. The GPU is then able to determine the effect the light will have on the object.

This can be seen in the following code.

```
glEnable(GL_LIGHTING)
glEnable(GL_LIGHT0)

# Set light properties
light_position = [1, 1, 1, 0]
light_color = [1, 1, 1, 1]
glLightfv(GL_LIGHT0, GL_POSITION, light_position)
glLightfv(GL_LIGHT0, GL_DIFFUSE, light_color)
glLightfv(GL_LIGHT0, GL_SPECULAR, light_color)
```

Here the colour of the light and its position can be altered to adjust how the lighting affects the objects onscreen.

8.3.2 Using uniforms to transform vertices

Uniforms were looked at in previous chapters. A uniform is simply a set of matrices that are written so that the values used to perform the calculations are unable to be changed within the program. The purpose of writing the calculation in this way is to allow other parts of the program to interact with the matrix without effecting other method statements or procedures. The matrix itself is written as a method and contains the information needed to perform the intended instruction. Below are a set of matrices used to perform calculations such as transformation and scale.

```
def scale(sx, sy, sz):
    scale_matrix = np.array([[sx, 0, 0, 0],
                             [0, sy, 0, 0],
                             [0, 0, sz, 0],
                             [0, 0, 0, 1]])
    glMultMatrixf(scale_matrix.T)

def translate(tx, ty, tz):
    translate_matrix = np.array([[1, 0, 0, tx],
                                 [0, 1, 0, ty],
                                 [0, 0, 1, tz],
                                 [0, 0, 0, 1]])
    glMultMatrixf(translate_matrix.T)

def rotate_x(angle):
    rad = np.radians(angle)
    rotate_matrix = np.array([[1, 0, 0, 0],
                              [0, np.cos(rad), -np.sin(rad), 0],
                              [0, np.sin(rad), np.cos(rad), 0],
                              [0, 0, 0, 1]])
    glMultMatrixf(rotate_matrix.T)
```

Adapting code within a program to apply hard written matrices often means writing separate files to contain the required information.

Summary of chapter

This chapter has examined how to create several types of procedures within OpenGL and how the code can appear within a graphical program. The GPU shares some of the tasks that the processor would usually complete during runtime, improving the overall performance of the software. Due to the design of the GPU, it is only possible to program the software so that it functions within the structure of the computer's hardware. The libraries that exist within OpenGL allow the processor to recognize the purpose of the algorithm.

End of Chapter Quiz

Describe how lighting is achieved in OpenGL

List several ways in which the GPU improves the operation of the program.

How are OpenGL files recognized?

What are the advantages of writing in OpenGL?

CHAPTER 9

Hardware design concepts

In this chapter, you will look at the following

- CPU vs GPU
- Rendering pipeline
- Threading and multicore
- Interpreting instructions

9.1.1 Rendering graphics with the GPU

The GPU is specifically designed to process data streams used for displaying graphical output. Writing code that utilizes the GPU can significantly improve the performance of a software application. This improvement occurs because the CPU alone cannot handle the same level of functionality as the graphics card. By allowing the GPU to perform certain tasks, the workload on the CPU is reduced during runtime. This means the GPU can effectively manage parts of the program, that require the rendering and processing of vector coordinates. Since the graphics card is built to handle these processes, integrating a graphics processor into the code can enhance the overall functionality of the program.

There are several assumptions that form the basis of the processes carried out by the GPU, many of which have been discussed in previous chapters. By understanding the conceptual frameworks within a 3D program, we can determine how a GPU processor is designed. Up to this point, the text has outlined the logical foundations of three-dimensional programming. Now, we will examine the functionality of the hardware and how the GPU executes a program's instructions.

9.1.2 Design of a graphics processor

Due to the intended purposes of the processor, the graphics card itself is integrated with the CPU and does not need to complete many of the functions of the central processor. This simplifies the design of the GPU into several essential tasks for the graphical I/O. Initial designs of the GPU allowed the processor to process binary into colour formats using an FPGA board as an output. The number of tasks has improved with further designs, allowing the GPU to complete tasks that were formerly carried out by the CPU. The aim of the text is only concerned with the design of 3D programs. For this reason, it will not be necessary to look at the structure of the FPGA. Instead, the text aims to define how the GPU can be developed to complete 3D routines.

HOW GPU PROCESSES DATA	
IMAGE RENDERING	Instruction processing
VECTOR PROCESSING	Data Loading
MULTITHREADING	Fragment Processing
PRIMITIVES ASSEMBLY	Rasterization

Table: 9.1.2 How the GPU Processes Data

9.2.1 The rendering pipeline

The data that passes through the graphics processor is arranged into a set number of stages that determine the flow of information. This means that a sequential logic system is needed that can handle the data and decode the instructions ready for the I/O. This is formerly called the rendering pipeline and allows the graphics card to prepare the data before processing the image. Without a coherent structure, the graphics card would be unable to process the algorithm. For instance, the rendering of an image requires the vectors to be calculated before the application of the 2D projected plane. Each event is required to occur in turn until the final data set is compiled and ready for completion. The order in which this is conducted is outlined below. It lists the stages in which the program is run.

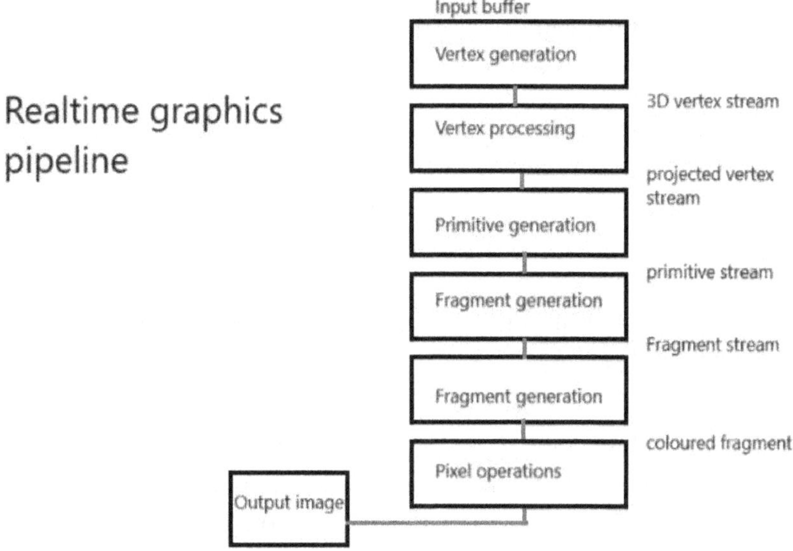

9.2.1 The rendering pipeline

The stages which define the structure of the program also relate to the hardware that exists in the GPU. The rendering pipeline designates how the code is compiled and the order in which the processor intends to move the data. This basic process starts with the calculation of the geometric coordinates to the rendering of the objects in the fragment shader. This coherence allows the program to successfully manipulate the data into a 2D image. This also infers how the hardware is designed and the type of logic required to achieve this process.

9.2.2 Coordination of software processes

The rendering process starts when the data is loaded for the current set of vertices, this is then updated against any transformation and passed to the fragment shader. This pattern occurs between each frame, loading the data before preparing the finished 2D image. The basic cycle determines how the routines of the program coincide so that the algorithm can coordinate the structures found within the processor. Due to the complexity of the GPU and the number of events that occur between each frame. It is necessary to understand the path that the program takes to coordinate the events in the processor. To better develop this concept it is possible to look at the layout and design of how the processor works.

9.2.3 initial layout of the graphics card

The structure of the GPU relies on the movement of data from the vertices into the fragment shader. The information is then recalculated according to the nature of the program. Any arithmetical functions needed for the data at this stage occur in the ALU. This includes the translation of coordinates; camera transforms and the stretching of textures to match the vertices. For this reason, the ALU found in the core has access to many of the structures within the GPU. Upon completion of recalculating the data, the information is then moved to the fragment shader. Here the primitives that describe the vertices are reordered according to the information in the Z_buffer. The information is then rendered and prepared for the final 2D image. The diagram below describes the basic layout for the GPU in terms of processing the image coordinates.

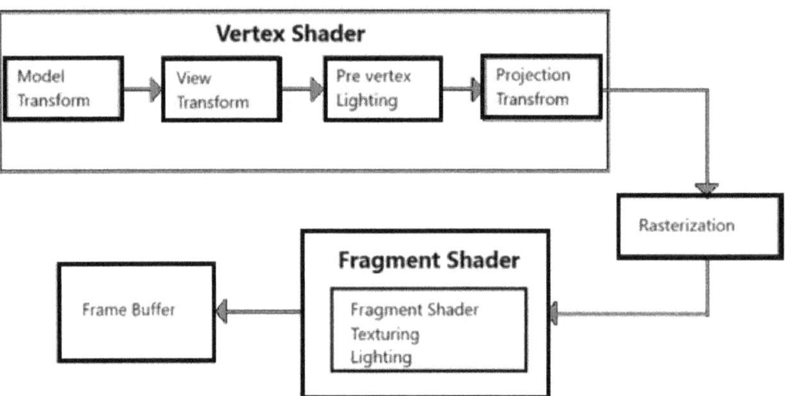

Fig: 9.2.3 Basic layout of the geometry shader

This is only a simplified version and does not include the processes involved in applying texture or light and shadow to an object. However, it is possible to determine how the data moves through the separate stages and some of the basic components required, to design the hardware.

HARDWARE STRUCTURES FOUND IN THE GPU	
PROCESSING UNITS (CUDA CORES)	Texture Units
MEMORY (VRAM)	Render Output Units
MEMORY CONTROLLERS	Cache Memory
SHADERS	Control Logic

Table: 9.1.2 List of components found in GPU hardware

9.3.1 Using multiple cores.

Due to the high volume of graphical data held within a single frame, The GPU has several cores that can work independently of each other. This is different from CPUs which might only have a single processor running at a higher clock speed. The advantages of such a system are that the processors can run tasks that include multiple data sets to process separate instructions. Modern graphical software often demands processing hundreds of polygons at the same time meaning the workload is required to be shared across many cores.

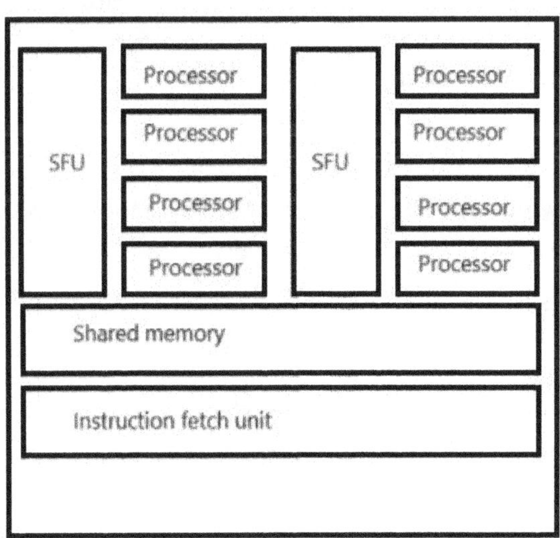

Fig 9.3.1 The structure of a single Multiprocessor

Inside the GPU the cores are split between multiprocessors, where a thousand cores might be split into a few hundred SM. This reduces the need to repeat instructions and uses something called a schedular to designate and run the simultaneous commands. This reduces the length of time to complete instructions and can handle more data simultaneously.

A single core might contain the following structures.

single-precision floating-point units function units (SFUs)
Schedulers for warps
A substantial number of registers (1000s)
Shared memory
Texture cache

These structures exist inside the GPU as it is designed to handle large amounts of graphical data.

9.3.2 Threading and multiple cores

Another advantage of the GPU is that it can decode a single instruction to a group of registers. This process is called threading. This means that a single core in a GPU can perform the same instruction up to ten times simultaneously. The core is built with several layers that all share the same structure. Each thread might contain 512 registers which are all able to process the same command from one instruction.

The following code represents a single instruction that the GPU might process simultaneously during one cycle.

```
def add_and_store(a, b):
    # Ensure inputs are numbers
    if not (isinstance(a, (int, float)) and isinstance(b, (int, float))):
        raise ValueError("Both 'a' and 'b' must be numbers.")

    # Perform addition and store result in 'c'
    c = a + b
    return c
```

```
# Example usage
a = 5
b = 10
c = add_and_store(a, b)
```

Here the registers A and B are added together and stored in a separate register C. Within a threading block this procedure can happen simultaneously within one processor up to ten times. Meaning that one instruction can be calculated across a series of registers. This is particularly important when updating the values used to store vectors, as the coordinates often appear as large data sets. The cores are designed in this way as single instructions are used on the data set. To change the values held for the vectors, without having to repeat the same process.

9.3.3 Example of threading program for GPU

Here is an example of a small piece of code that describes how the GPU creates a calculation across a series of registers. The program takes 1024 random numbers simultaneously and multiplies them against another set of random values. The code describes how the GPU can load the information into a single block of memory and perform the calculation on the two sets of data.

```
# CUDA kernel as a string
kernel_code = “”””
__global__ void add_vectors(float *a, float *b, float *c, int n)
{int idx = threadIdx.x + blockDim.x * blockIdx.x;
   if (idx < n) {
      c[idx] = a[idx] + b[idx];}}”””

# Compile the kernel code
mod = SourceModule(kernel_code)

# Get the kernel function
add_vectors = mod.get_function(“add_vectors”)
```

```
# Initialize the data
N = 1024
a = np.random.randn(N).astype(np.float32)
b = np.random.randn(N).astype(np.float32)
c = np.zeros_like(a)

# Allocate memory on the GPU
a_gpu = drv.mem_alloc(a.nbytes)
b_gpu = drv.mem_alloc(b.nbytes)
c_gpu = drv.mem_alloc(c.nbytes)

# Transfer data to the GPU
drv.memcpy_htod(a_gpu, a)
drv.memcpy_htod(b_gpu, b)

# Execute the kernel
block_size = 256
grid_size = (N + block_size - 1) // block_size
add_vectors(a_gpu, b_gpu, c_gpu, np.int32(N), block=(block_size, 1, 1),
grid=(grid_size, 1))

# Transfer the result back to the CPU
drv.memcpy_dtoh(c, c_gpu)

# Print the result
print("Vector a:", a)
print("Vector b:", b)
print("Vector c (result):", c)
```

9.3.4 Interpreting Instructions on the GPU

The processor inside the graphics card handles instructions in a similar method to that found within the CPU. The processor is still required to decode the instruction and move information around the system in binary. To better understand this process it is necessary to look at a few codes written in ASM that explain how a calculation might occur within machine language. As ASM is closer to how the circuit is designed, it is possible to understand the type of logic used to build the circuits.

Here is a short code to add two vectors together using ASM.

```
// Assuming v1 and v2 are the two vectors (each with x and y components)
// Result is stored in the vector result (also with x and y components)

// Load the vector components into registers
ld.param.f32 %f1, [v1_x];
ld.param.f32 %f2, [v1_y];
ld.param.f32 %f3, [v2_x];
ld.param.f32 %f4, [v2_y];

// Perform the addition
add.f32 %f5, %f1, %f3; // result_x = v1_x + v2_x
add.f32 %f6, %f2, %f4; // result_y = v1_y + v2_y

// Store the result
st.param.f32 [result_x], %f5;
st.param.f32 [result_y], %f6;
```

From the code, it is possible to determine that the registers in the GPU can be accessed to store binary. A simple procedure is used to calculate the code and store the result in a separate register.

Summary of chapter

The chapter has looked again at the rendering pipeline, looking at the movement of data and how the hardware within the GPU is designed. As the processor is integrated into the CPU, the two components share many of the same procedures. By understanding how the hardware works and identifying the components inside the graphics card. It is possible to develop code that can work with the CPU to process visual and graphical data.

End of Chapter Quiz

Identify three components of the graphics card

Describe how the fragment shader works

Draw a flow diagram of the flow of data in the GPU

What process initiates the movement of data in the GPU?

CHAPTER 10

GPU structures and hardware

In this chapter, you will look at the following

- Identify circuitry in GPU
- The processor and loading instructions
- The ALU
- Structures in the fragment shader

10.1.1 Circuit design of the GPU

As the GPU is integrated into other structures within the computer, the circuitry within the GPU is similar in design and uses the same procedures. For instance, the instruction set uses the same methods of binary to perform operations, and the ALU has a similar type of arithmetic decoder. Most of the processes that are used to create a 3D application can be completed on the CPU. Meaning, that it is possible to design a graphics card based on these similar principles. This chapter looks at how 3D graphic routines are completed by the hardware in the device, and also the design of the systems required.

10.1.2 The processor and ALU

A processor decodes an instruction held in the instruction register and performs the command in a series of stages. This is called the fetch-execute cycle. This process determines how the processor moves the instruction across the data bus, to carry out the procedure. The most basic instructions often include the ALU. These types of commands simply load a set of data into the register and perform a calculation based on the current instruction. To better understand how this process works it is possible to look at how a routine is called in the ALU.

Here is a simple code to find the sum of two values

```
section .data
  num1 dd 5 ; First number
  num2 dd 10 ; Second number
  result dd 0 ; Result of the operation

section .text
  global _start

_start:
  ; Load the numbers into registers
  mov eax, [num1] ; Load num1 into EAX
  mov ebx, [num2] ; Load num2 into EBX

  ; Perform an operation using the ALU (e.g., addition)
  add eax, ebx ; EAX = EAX + EBX

  ; Store the result
  mov [result], eax ; Store the result back to memory

  ; Exit (Linux syscall)
  mov eax, 1 ; syscall number (sys_exit)
  xor ebx, ebx ; exit code 0
  int 0x80 ; interrupt to invoke syscall
```

As can be seen, the program simply loads the values into a set of registers, using the add routine to perform the calculation inside the ALU. This procedure would be used within a GPU and describes how the processor can complete calculations on the values that are held for the geometric data.

10.1.3 Design of a simple processor

The processors found within the GPU are similar to those found in the computers structure. They share a similar range of components which are used to fetch and decode the instructions sent to the GPU. As the information is held in the system memory, the GPU decodes each instruction being sent from the processor, before updating the program counter. This allows the GPU to time each command being sent from the central processor. The GPU then decodes each instruction and allows the control unit to determine the flow of data.

Once the data is loaded onto the bus the instruction register will determine how the opcode is expected to be performed by the ALU. Once this process is complete the next instruction will be loaded into the instruction register.

Example of a fetch execute cycle

Instruction Fetch
Instruction Decode
Operand Fetch
Instruction Dispatch
Execution
Write Back
Program Counter Update
Memory Access

This procedure is similar to the events that occur within the CPU except the program counter is controlled externally. Also the fetch cycle also includes events to update the registers and memory. As well as processing commands that include batch data. As the processors themselves appear as a series of cores. The GPU has to interpret each instruction simultaneously across the sperate cores.

10.2.1 complex tasks that include projection

The fragment shader uses a component called the depth or Z_buffer to determine elements of shading and projection. This is a series of registers that hold the depth values for the pixels on the screen. How this works is that once the shapes have been drawn into primitives and projected as a 2D image, the values that are held in the vectors are kept to determine the distance on screen. This allows the projected image to identify which objects are in front, and the colours used within the fragment shader.

The code below describes a simple procedure to identify the range of a pixel determined by the information held in the depth buffer.

```
; Input: Pixel position and depth
; Output: Color if pixel is in foreground, discard otherwise

; Pseudocode for fragment shader
main:
  ; Load pixel position
  MOV R0, pixel_position
  ; Load depth value of current pixel
  MOV R1, depth_value
  ; Load depth buffer value at pixel position

  TEX R2, R0, depth_buffer
  ; Compare current pixel depth with depth buffer value
  CMP R3, R1, R2 ; R3 = (R1 < R2) ? 1 : 0

  ; If R3 is 1, the current pixel is in the foreground
  IF R3 == 1:
    ; Output the color of the pixel (foreground color)
    MOV output_color, foreground_color
  ELSE:
    ; Discard the pixel (background)
    DISCARD

  ; End of shader program
  END
```

As can be seen from the program the routine can be completed by a standard processor. Although the GPU uses a depth buffer to improve the performance of this particular task.

10.2.2 Render output unit (ROP)

Another stage of the fragment shader is the rendering of texture onto individual polygons. Again this is a simple procedure of reformatting a texture file into a new position according to the evaluation of the object's shape on a 2D plane. The image is redrawn according to the ratio of the number of pixels that occur for each side given for the shape.

The program below identifies how this task is completed using a set of small routines.

```
# Texture coordinates
tex_coords = [(0, 0), (1, 0),
  (1, 1), (0, 1)]

# Function to project 3D points to 2D
def project_point(point, scale=300, offset=(width//2, height//2)):
  x = int(point[0] * scale + offset[0])
  y = int(-point[1] * scale + offset[1])
  return x, y
# Function to draw textured faces
def draw_textured_faces(faces, vertices, tex_coords, texture):
  for face in faces:
    face_vertices = [vertices[i] for i in face]
    points_2d = [project_point(v) for v in face_vertices]
    # Create a surface for the face
    face_surface = pygame.Surface((256, 256))
    face_surface.blit(texture, (0, 0))

    # Map the texture onto the face
    tex_points = [(tc[0] * 256, tc[1] * 256) for tc in tex_coords]
    pygame.draw.polygon(screen, black, points_2d, 0)
    pygame.transform.scale(face_surface, (points_2d[2][0] - points_
2d[0][0], points_2d[2][1] - points_2d[0][1]))
    pygame.gfxdraw.textured_polygon(screen, points_2d, face_surface,
0, 0)
```

Here the image is rescaled according to the new position of the objects shape. This occurs because the hardware can group pixels and resize units within the image in a similar way that scale is achieved within an ordinary computer program. The object's new dimensions affect how the texture is drawn onto the polygon's shape.

10.2.3 Using lighting and ray caster modules

Ray-caster lighting can be completed by the hardware within the GPU in a simple process of altering the colour used to determine shapes. This occurs because a point is given for a light source and a simple procedure determines at what point the ray hits the given object. Any points that are in the same location as the object alter the shader used to render the image.

Here is a procedure to create a raycaster within a given program.

```
section .data
screen_width equ 320
screen_height equ 200
map_width equ 24
map_height equ 24

section .bss
buffer resb screen_width * screen_height
section .text
global _start

_start:
; Initialization code; Assuming video mode is already set (e.g., 13h mode)

main_loop:
; Raycasting logic here; Loop through each column of the screen
mov ecx, screen_width
mov esi, buffer
```

```
cast_rays:
; Ray direction and calculation code here; Draw pixel in buffer
mov [esi], al
inc esi
loop cast_rays
; Render the buffer to the screen
mov edx, screen_height
mov esi, buffer

render_screen:
; Write buffer to video memory
mov edi, 0xA0000
mov ecx, screen_width
rep movsb
dec edx
jnz render_screen

; Check for user input to exit loop or continue; Loop to keep updating the screen
jmp main_loop
```

How the program works, is that the original coordinates loop through the x and y axis changing one pixel at a time, determining if the value in the depth buffer indicates that the ray has reached an object. Each iteration changes pattern depending on the angle given for the ray. This is a simple procedure that can be completed by the graphics card using a raycaster module, which can be used to add secondary light sources.

Summary of chapter

The chapter has identified some of the hardware that is required to run a 3D program. These structures have been explained using code to offer a better understanding of how these types of units are designed. Due to the GPU being integrated into a normal processor, the GPU shares many of the same structures. Although, it is necessary to point out that the GPU is expected to simultaneously perform thousands of calculations per second. For this reason, the GPU uses hundreds of cores to modify and process the data.

End of Chapter Quiz

Design a simple GPU structure using diagrams.

Create a flowchart of code moving through the GPU

How would a texture mapping unit be designed?

List some other circuits used in the GPU.

PART 3

Programming for 3D applications

CHAPTER 11

Designing a simple 3D environment

In this chapter, you will look at the following

- Creating geometric shapes
- Using uniforms for movement and rotation
- Creating methods for perspective and camera movement
- Running a program

11.1.1 Designing a simple games engine

This chapter and those that follow will contain some working examples of how a games engine can be created through basic hard written code. The idea is to explore some of the ideas and concepts that have been used in the text, with a few programs that demonstrate how the ideas work. The task of creating a 3D space within a program comprises of a number of mathematical principles and logic that at first seem overly complex. The intention of the text has been to allow the reader the chance to familiarise themselves with the topic and allow them to understand the conventions used within programming. The chapter explores how these ideas can be developed within code.

11.1.2 Initialising the window

Writing a program begins by declaring a few statements that initialise the screen and the libraries that the code uses. This allows the program to format the output for the display, and determine what extensions are needed for the code to run. It is also possible at this stage to declare any variables and constants that the code will use later on in the program. For example.

```
import pygame
import numpy as np
from math import sin, cos, radians
import random

pygame.init()
screenWidth = 600
screenHeight = 600

# Define colors
white = (255, 255, 255)
black = (0, 0, 0)
red = (255, 0, 0)

#init screen
screen = pygame.display.set_mode((screenWidth,screenHeight))
pygame.display.set_caption("3D program")
clock = pygame.time.Clock()

# Fill the background with white
screen.fill(white)
```

Here the code lists the intended libraries used, and the parameters needed for the output of the display.

11.1.3 Creating a geometric model

Designing a 3D object is a simple process of drawing a volumetric shape across three axes. This can be completed in a number of ways depending on how the code draws the polygons and creates the movement for the object. The following example lists the dimensions of a cube across three axes.

```
x = [-1,1,1,-1,-1,1,1,-1]
y = [-1,-1,1,1,-1,-1,1,1]
z = [1,1,1,1,-1,-1,-1,-1]
```

This principle demonstrates how a set of coordinates can be created out of a simple list that states the objects dimensions. Within a program a set of objects can be created by adding further lists with other coordinates.

11.2.1 Movement and rotation

The formulas for creating geometric translations have been mentioned in previous chapters. Within a program it is possible to write these expressions as a constant that the program can use each time it is called. This way the method is then able to change the position of the camera or the object, without effecting the information used within the formula. For example the following method allows a set of coordinates to be rotated depending on the angle presented inside the declaration.

```
def rotate_x(angle):
    rad = np.radians(angle)
    rotate_matrix = np.array([[1, 0, 0, 0],
                        [0, np.cos(rad), -np.sin(rad), 0],
                        [0, np.sin(rad), np.cos(rad), 0],
                        [0, 0, 0, 1]]
```

Depending on the intention of the program, this method can be used for repositioning an object or the coordinates used to describe the world view. Other types of constants include translations and scale which can all be written as methods that the program is able to then draw upon.

```
def translate(tx, ty, tz):
    translate_matrix = np.array([[1, 0, 0, tx],
                        [0, 1, 0, ty],
                        [0, 0, 1, tz],
                        [0, 0, 0, 1]])
```

11.3.1 Perspective and 2D projection

The final types of method needed to create the virtual environment are a few formulas to create the objects perspective and camera movement. This can be completed as a simple formula that the objects coordinates pass through after assuming any movement on screen. For example the following code should be enough to demonstrate a typical field of view on a 3D shape.

```
def project(x, y, z, distance):
factor = distance / (distance + z)
x_proj = x * factor
y_proj = y * factor
return x_proj, y_proj
```

This code should provide a simple method of redetermining a 3D coordinate to a 2D perspective.

11.3.2 Camera movement

The movement of the camera redetermines the location of each of the objects found onscreen. This means that the coordinates held within the world view will be redetermined by any movement affecting the camera. To achieve this a transform is used to update the world view each time the camera changes position. For example

```
def translate(camerX, camerY, camerZ):
    camera[0] =+ camerX
    camera[1] =+ camerY
    camera[2] =+ camerZ

    for i in range(len(x)):
    #a = [xg[i], yg[i], zg[i]]
    xpp = xg[i] + camera[0]
    ypp = yg[i] + camera[1]
    zpp = zg[i] + camera[2]
    [xg[i], yg[i], zg[i]] = [xpp, ypp, zpp]
```

Here the coordinates within the model are redetermined by the movement that occurs within the camera.

11.4.1 Running the program

Once the methods used within the program have been written it is possible to write a small while loop that runs through each process in turn. This involves stating each method in order and declaring any event handlers that occur during the program. Depending on the intended behaviour of the program it is also necessary to add a timer to process how the program updates between each frame.

Summary of chapter

The chapter has explored how a simple program can be written to create objects within a virtual environment. This process is explained only at a basic level that incorporates a few procedures. More complex 3D engines require more detail to design as they tend to include other aspects such as detailed lighting and rendering. Although the principle used to design the program is similar to the methods mentioned here. The rest of the text will look at examples of 3D problems.

End of Chapter Quiz

Write a program for rotating an object.

How is camera rotation called during a program?

What types of procedure use constants?

List the dimensions for a 3D shape.

CHAPTER 12

Designing a rotating cube

In this chapter, you will look at the following

- How to design a simple program
- Principles of perspective and rotation
- Model coordinates

12.1.1 Designing a program for a rotating cube

The chapter will look at the implementation and design of writing a program to create a rotating cube. The intention is to better understand some of the processes described throughout the text. The program itself draws a cube onto the screen and rotates each of the coordinates so that the cube appears to rotate within the centre of the window. The code uses several techniques to reposition the coordinates and create a sense of perspective in the 3D image.

12.1.2 Flow chart to describe the program

The diagram below describes the flowchart for writing a program to create an image of a rotating cube. The program starts by creating the method statements for the cube and designing a 3D set of vectors to position the coordinates. The routine draws the cube and rotates the values within the vectors according to the rotational matrix. The angle is increased, and the program loops back to the object's new position, repeating the process.

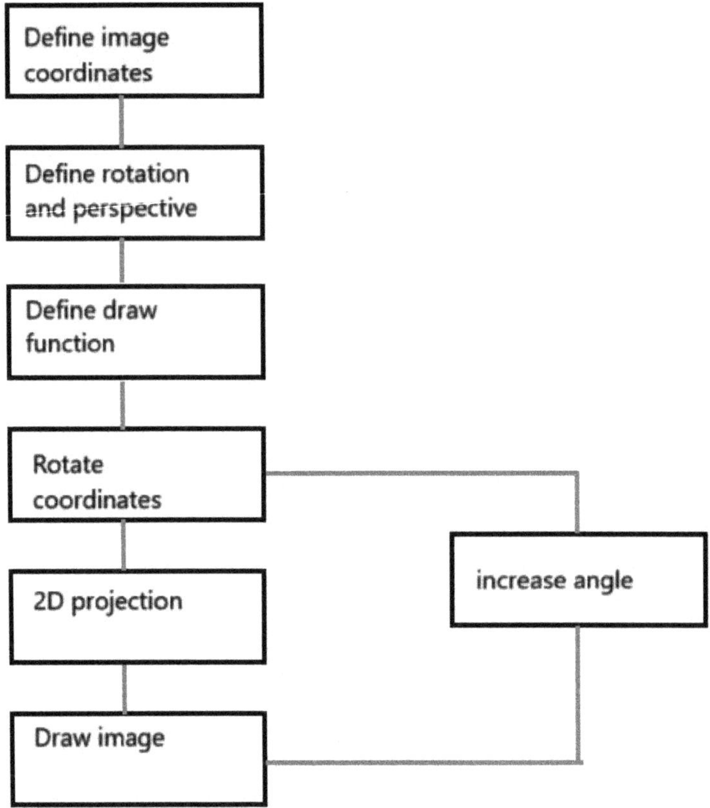

Fig: 12.1.2 Basic flowchart for the design of the program

12.2.1 Creating the vectors for the image

The cube starts as a set of vectors that determine the position of each of the points listed within the cube. This is seen as the following list.

x = [-1,1,1,-1,-1,1,1,-1]
y = [-1,-1,1,1,-1,-1,1,1]
z = [1,1,1,1,-1,-1,-1,-1]

A single point will be found within the list in the following format.

A = x[0],y[0],z[0] = -1,-1,1

This is used to describe the model. The points are drawn onto the screen by multiplying the coordinates by a scale of 100 and adding the value to the x and y positions for the centre of the screen. This keeps the image bound within the middle of the output window. A point to note is that the values contain positive and negative values, so the points used to describe the object can turn towards themselves during each rotation. This procedure is typical for creating a rotation within the model viewpoint.

12.2.2 Rotation and perspective

The rotation and perspective calculations are achieved by multiplying each point that is used to describe the cube, by a series of matrix transformations. These have been identified previously within the text, although the formula used for the perspective is a slightly more complicated version. It uses a number of procedures to identify the distance of the furthest plane. For instance, the following matrices are used for the purpose of rotation.

A = [x,y,z]
x = [cos(angle), 0, sin(angle)]
y = [0, 1, 0]
z = [-sin(angle), 0, cos(angle)]

During the program, each point is multiplied by the value held within the matrix, where the angle is the current value for the variable within the system.

12.3.1 Running the routine

Running the program should produce an output of a 3D image of a cube rotating in the centre of the screen. The image that is produced should also allow for a sense of perspective to allow the coordinates to be identified by the distance from the viewer. The image is drawn by processing an algorithm that determines the points of each line according to the 2D projection of the object's point.

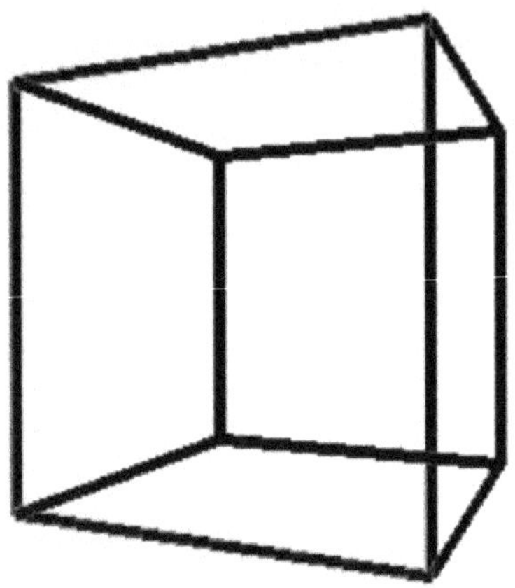

Fig: 12.3.1 Output for program

```
import pygame
import numpy as np
from math import sin, cos, radians

pygame.init()
screenWidth = 600
screenHeight = 600

# Define colors
white = (255, 255, 255)
black = (0, 0, 0)
red = (255, 0, 0)

#init screen
screen = pygame.display.set_mode((screenWidth,screenHeight))
pygame.display.set_caption("Rotate Example")

clock = pygame.time.Clock()

# Fill the background with white
screen.fill(white)
```

```
x = [-1,1,1,-1,-1,1,1,-1]
y = [-1,-1,1,1,-1,-1,1,1]
z = [1,1,1,1,-1,-1,-1,-1]

#global coordinates
xg = [0,1,2,3,4,5,6,7]
yg = [0,1,2,3,4,5,6,7]
zg = [0,1,2,3,4,5,6,7]

scale = 150
pos = 300

# Draw a black line between the points
#pygame.draw.line(screen, black, start_point, end_point, 5)

# Update the display
pygame.display.flip()

def persepctive(xfp, yfp, zfp):
  for i in range(len(x)):
    a = xg[i] - xfp
    b = yg[i] - yfp
    c = zg[i] +abs(zfp)
    q = np.sqrt(a*a+b*b+c*c)
    ux = a/q
    uy = b/q
    uz = c/q
    qh = q*abs(zfp)/(zg[i] + abs(zfp))
    xh = ux*qh+xfp
    yh = uy*qh+yfp
    zh = uz*qh+zfp
    xg[i] = xh
    yg[i] = yh
    zg[i] = zh
```

```
def rotate(angle):
    for i in range(len(x)):
        a = [x[i], y[i], z[i]]
        b = [cos(angle), 0, sin(angle)]
        xpp = np.inner(a,b)
        b = [0, 1, 0]
        ypp = np.inner(a,b)
        b = [-sin(angle), 0, cos(angle)]
        zpp = np.inner(a,b)
        [xg[i], yg[i], zg[i]] = [xpp*scale+pos, ypp*scale+pos, zpp*scale+pos]

def drawBox():
    pygame.draw.line(screen, red, (xg[3], yg[3]),(xg[0], yg[0]), 5)
    pygame.draw.line(screen, black, (xg[3], yg[3]),(xg[7], yg[7]), 5)
    pygame.draw.line(screen, black, (xg[7], yg[7]),(xg[4], yg[4]), 5)
    pygame.draw.line(screen, black, (xg[4], yg[4]),(xg[0], yg[0]), 5)
    pygame.draw.line(screen, red, (xg[3], yg[3]),(xg[2], yg[2]), 5)
    pygame.draw.line(screen, black, (xg[7], yg[7]),(xg[6], yg[6]), 5)
    pygame.draw.line(screen, black, (xg[5], yg[5]),(xg[4], yg[4]), 5)
    pygame.draw.line(screen, red, (xg[1], yg[1]),(xg[0], yg[0]), 5)
    pygame.draw.line(screen, red, (xg[2], yg[2]),(xg[1], yg[1]), 5)
    pygame.draw.line(screen, black, (xg[1], yg[1]),(xg[5], yg[5]), 5)
    pygame.draw.line(screen, black, (xg[5], yg[5]),(xg[6], yg[6]), 5)
    pygame.draw.line(screen, black, (xg[6], yg[6]),(xg[2], yg[2]), 5)

xfp = 200
yfp = 200
zfp = 160
#persepctive(xfp, yfp, zfp)

#extent of rotation
angle = 0
angle += 0.01

while True:
    screen.fill((255,255,255))
```

```
    rotate(angle)
    persepctive(300,300,300)
    drawBox()
    angle += 0.01

for event in pygame.event.get():
    if event.type == pygame.QUIT:
        pygame.quit()
        quit()

    pygame.display.update()
    clock.tick(180)
```

Summary of chapter

The chapter has identified how to run a simple program to create a 3D model. The process can be achieved by simply stating a set of vectors and manipulating the coordinates so that the object appears to move and be repositioned. The program looked at creating perspective and using matrices to determine the position of coordinates.

End of Chapter Quiz

Write a simple set of coordinates to design an object.

How are matrices used to reposition objects?

How are the 2D points found for a vector?

Design a simple procedure to unpack a set of polygons.

CHAPTER 13

A series of cubes

In this chapter, you will look at the following

- How to design a simple program
- Initialising a class object
- Setting up a camera

13.1.1 Designing a program for a series of rotating cubes

The chapter is going to look at writing another program for rotating a cube in 3D. The difference is that the program draws several cubes simultaneously and includes the use of camera movement. The code demonstrates how the computer might coordinate the process of repositioning the location of more than one set of vectors. There is also a set of inputs that allow the user to navigate through the program and move the position of the camera. Enabling the cubes to be viewed from any number of angles.

13.1.2 Flow chart to describe the program

The flowchart illustrates how the program is designed to update during each frame. The code used in this example is similar to that of the previous program, but it now includes a new user input for controlling the movement of the camera. Additionally, the camera requires its own method to adjust the viewing angle. The user input functions through an event handler that updates the camera's position and angle. This mechanism allows the routine to be interrupted, changing the variable that determines the camera's position.

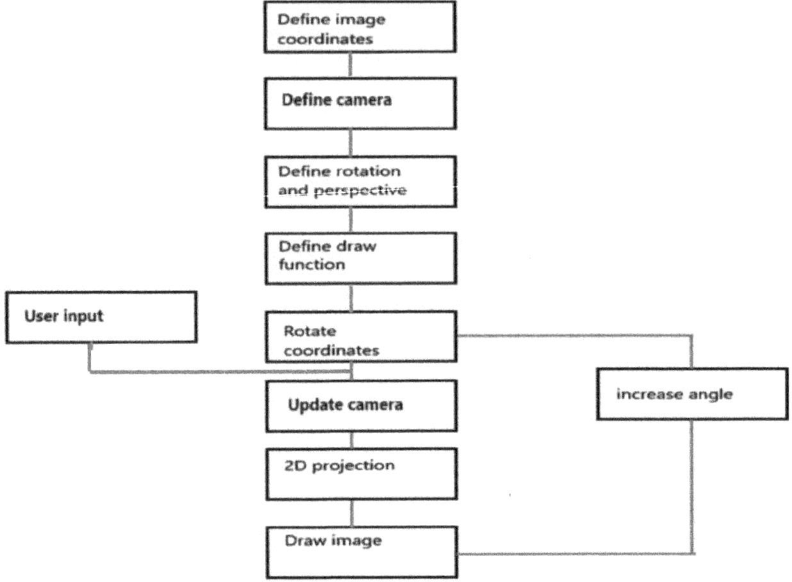

Fig: 13.1.2 Flowchart for random cubes

13.2.1 Initializing an object for the cubes

The cubes are drawn onto the screen in a random set of locations each time the program is called. This occurs by creating a list of cubes that each have a series of vectors to describe the shape. The cubes are written as an object with their own set of procedures. This allows the program to initialize the object and create the parameters for the cubes at the start of the program. This simply allocates a new dataset containing the parameters each time it is called. The object can return several methods that allow the program to alter the position and rotation of the cubes.

13.2.2 Setting up a camera

The view from the camera is able to be moved to reposition how the images appear on the screen. This is controlled by the values provided by the user input, which updates the variables used to describe the object. The method to create this procedure is written below.

```
def translate(camerX, camerY, camerZ):
  camera[0] =+ camerX
  camera[1] =+ camerY
  camera[2] =+ camerZ

  for i in range(len(x)):
    xpp = xg[i] + camera[0]
    ypp = yg[i] + camera[1]
    zpp = zg[i] + camera[2]
    [xg[i], yg[i], zg[i]] = [xpp, ypp, zpp]
```

During the program, the vectors held in the list of cubes are updated with the new coordinates provided by the movement of the camera. The function loops through each vector in the list altering the current position used to describe the cubes' location. The translation of the camera coordinates creates the appearance of movement from the objects on the screen.

13.3.1 Running the routine

The program should create a series of cubes that appear in a random position each time the code is called. The cubes rotate within a 3D plane. Moving the camera angle of the point of view is also possible. The diagram below is taken from the program and indicates how the program is intended to run.

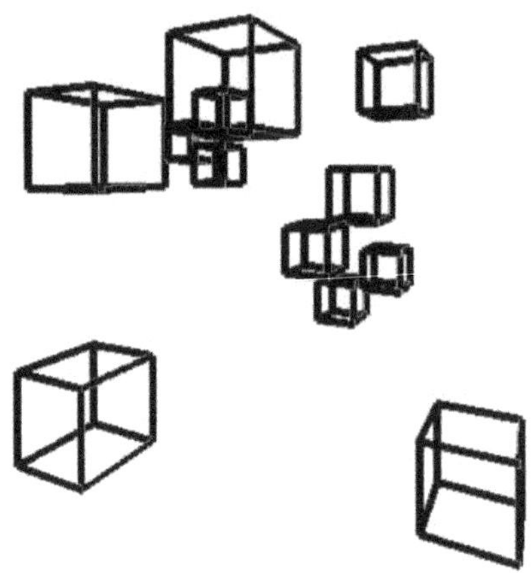

Fig: 13.3.1 Repeating set of cubes

```
import pygame
import numpy as np
from math import sin, cos, radians
import random

pygame.init()

screenWidth = 600
screenHeight = 600

# Define colors
white = (255, 255, 255)
black = (0, 0, 0)
red = (255, 0, 0)

#init screen
screen = pygame.display.set_mode((screenWidth,screenHeight))
pygame.display.set_caption("Rotate Example")
clock = pygame.time.Clock()

# Fill the background with white
screen.fill(white)
```

```
x = [-1,1,1,-1,-1,1,1,-1]
y = [-1,-1,1,1,-1,-1,1,1]
z = [1,1,1,1,-1,-1,-1,-1]

#global coordinates
xg = [0,1,2,3,4,5,6,7]
yg = [0,1,2,3,4,5,6,7]
zg = [0,1,2,3,4,5,6,7]

# Update the display
pygame.display.flip()

class island():
  def __init__(self):
    self.scale = 50
    self.posX = -125
    self.posY = 25
    self.posZ = 100
    self.numberofIslands = 12
    self.island_list = []

  def initialize_islands(self):
    for i in range(self.numberofIslands):
        self.posX = random.randint(1, 580)
        self.posY = random.randint(1, 580)
        self.posZ = random.randint(1, 1500)
        self.island_list.append([self.scale, self.posX, self.posY, self.posZ])

  def rotateX(self, angle):
    for j in range(self.numberofIslands):
        for i in range(len(x)):
        a = [x[i], y[i], z[i]]
        b = [cos(angle), 0, sin(angle)]
        xpp = np.inner(a,b)
        b = [0, 1, 0]
        ypp = np.inner(a,b)
        b = [-sin(angle), 0, cos(angle)]
```

```
            zpp = np.inner(a,b)
            [xg[i], yg[i], zg[i]] = [xpp*self.island_list[j][0] +self.island_list[j]
[1], ypp*self.island_list[j][0]+self.island_list[j][2], zpp*self.island_list[j]
[0]+self.island_list[j][3]]

            translate(camerX, camerY, camerZ)
            persepctive(300,300,300)
            drawBox()

def persepctive(xfp, yfp, zfp):

   for i in range(len(x)):
      a = xg[i] - xfp
      b = yg[i] - yfp
      c = zg[i] +abs(zfp)
      q = np.sqrt(a*a+b*b+c*c)
      ux = a/q
      uy = b/q
      uz = c/q
      qh = q*abs(zfp)/(zg[i] + abs(zfp))
      xh = ux*qh+xfp
      yh = uy*qh+yfp
      zh = uz*qh+zfp
      xg[i] = xh
      yg[i] = yh
      zg[i] = zh

   def translate(camerX, camerY, camerZ):
      camera[0] =+ camerX
      camera[1] =+ camerY
      camera[2] =+ camerZ

      for i in range(len(x)):
        #a = [xg[i], yg[i], zg[i]]
        xpp = xg[i] + camera[0]
        ypp = yg[i] + camera[1]
        zpp = zg[i] + camera[2]
```

```
        [xg[i], yg[i], zg[i]] = [xpp, ypp, zpp]

    def drawScale(scale, posX, posY, posZ):
      for i in range(len(x)):
      a = [x[i], y[i], z[i]]
      xpp = x[i]
      ypp = y[i]
      zpp = z[i]
          [xg[i], yg[i], zg[i]] = [(xpp*scale)+posX, (ypp*scale)+posY,
(zpp*scale)+posZ]

def drawBox():
    pygame.draw.line(screen, red, (xg[3], yg[3]),(xg[0], yg[0]), 5)
    pygame.draw.line(screen, black, (xg[3], yg[3]),(xg[7], yg[7]), 5)
    pygame.draw.line(screen, black, (xg[7], yg[7]),(xg[4], yg[4]), 5)
    pygame.draw.line(screen, black, (xg[4], yg[4]),(xg[0], yg[0]), 5)
    pygame.draw.line(screen, red, (xg[3], yg[3]),(xg[2], yg[2]), 5)
    pygame.draw.line(screen, black, (xg[7], yg[7]),(xg[6], yg[6]), 5)
    pygame.draw.line(screen, black, (xg[5], yg[5]),(xg[4], yg[4]), 5)
    pygame.draw.line(screen, red, (xg[1], yg[1]),(xg[0], yg[0]), 5)
    pygame.draw.line(screen, red, (xg[2], yg[2]),(xg[1], yg[1]), 5)
    pygame.draw.line(screen, black, (xg[1], yg[1]),(xg[5], yg[5]), 5)
    pygame.draw.line(screen, black, (xg[5], yg[5]),(xg[6], yg[6]), 5)
    pygame.draw.line(screen, black, (xg[6], yg[6]),(xg[2], yg[2]), 5)

angle = 0
camera = [0,0,0]
camerX = 150
camerY = 100
camerZ = 100

world1 = island()
world1.initialize_islands()

while True:
    screen.fill((255,255,255))
    world1.rotateX(angle)
```

```
    angle += 0.01

    for event in pygame.event.get():
        if event.type == pygame.QUIT:
        pygame.quit()
        quit()
if event.type == pygame.KEYDOWN:
    if event.key == pygame.K_LEFT:
        angle += 0.1
    elif event.key == pygame.K_RIGHT:
        angle += -0.1
    if event.key == pygame.K_a:
        camerX += 35
    elif event.key == pygame.K_d:
        camerX += -35
    elif event.key == pygame.K_UP:
        camerY += 35
    elif event.key == pygame.K_DOWN:
        camerY += -35
    elif event.key == pygame.K_w:
        camerZ += -35
    elif event.key == pygame.K_s:
        camerZ += 35
    elif event.key == pygame.K_1:
        del world1.island_list[0]
        world1.numberofIslands -= 1

 pygame.display.update()
 clock.tick(180)
```

Summary of chapter

The program demonstrates a number of ways in which 3D graphics can be achieved within an application, as well as the type of concepts needed. Working in 3D involves a number of stages that define the properties of the models and the projection of the images onto a 2D plane. The chapter has aimed to provide an example of how this can be completed when writing a simple program.

End of Chapter Quiz

How are methods written when defining new objects?

Describe how 3D objects are created on a 2D plane.

Write your code for a rotating 3D cube.

Explain what would occur without projection.

CHAPTER 14

Creating a polygon unpacker

In this chapter, you will look at the following

- How to design a simple program
- Writing the dimensions for a single mesh
- Creating a loop to draw a set of polygons

14.1.1 Writing the code to create a 2D polygon unpacker

The purpose of the chapter is to define a method for drawing a series of 2D coordinates. This type of example is useful to the design of producing complex meshes which are able to recreate the structure of 3D objects. How the program works is by looping through the dimensions of a set of vertices that are used to describe a simple 2D shape. The shape itself is made from a number of polygons that the program draws in turn during each iteration of the loop. The intention is to describe the process which is used to draw a set of polygons, and reduce the amount of code needed to write the iteration. This process is important as It is possible to use this same procedure when designing an object that uses a larger range of polygonal coordinates.

14.1.2 Flow chart to describe the program

The program used to draw the polygons is quite simple as the program merely draws each shape in turn, creating the final 2D image. How this is achieved is through defining the coordinates of each polygon and using a loop to draw the shape as a series of 2D lines. This procedure is completed for each of the polygons held in the list that describes the shape. The program then loops through each time a change in the program occurs. It is important to note that the list that holds the coordinates needs to clearly state the dimensions for the shape, separating each of the image's polygons.

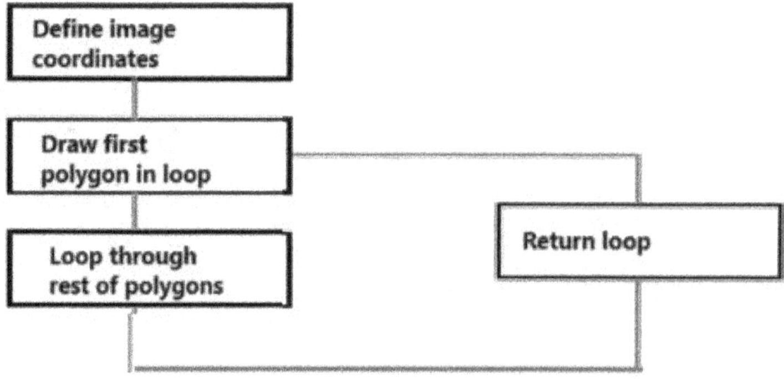

Fig: 14.1.2 flow chart for a polygon unpacker

14.2.1 Creating the shapes coordinates

The shape itself is a set of four triangle polygons. During the program the coordinates are written as a set of x and y vectors that describe the points of each part of the polygon. The list is written as a series of parts that are separated for each individual polygon. This allows the program to differentiate each of the coordinates in turn. The list below describes how this is written inside the program.

```
polygons = [[[100, 300,], [300, 300,], [100, 300,]],
        [[100, 300,], [300, 500,], [300, 300,]],
        [[300, 100,], [500, 300,], [500, 300,]],
        [[300, 500,], [300, 300,], [500, 300,]],]
```

As can be seen the shape has a list of four polygons with three individual coordinates.

14.2.2 Drawing the outline for the shape

To draw the shape the program draws a line between each of the coordinates in turn. How this is achieved is that the program loops through the list and uses the reference points to determine the coordinates for a group of simple lines. This procedure allows the program to draw the first polygon and repeat the pattern for each of the polygons contained in the list.

14.3.1 Running the program

The output from the program should create a 2D square made from a series of triangle polygons. The diagram below details how this should look within the program. It is important to note that the purpose of the code is to use a loop which can be designed to reduce the code and simplify the procedure for drawing a complicated mesh. As can be seen the square itself appears at 45 degrees from the base.

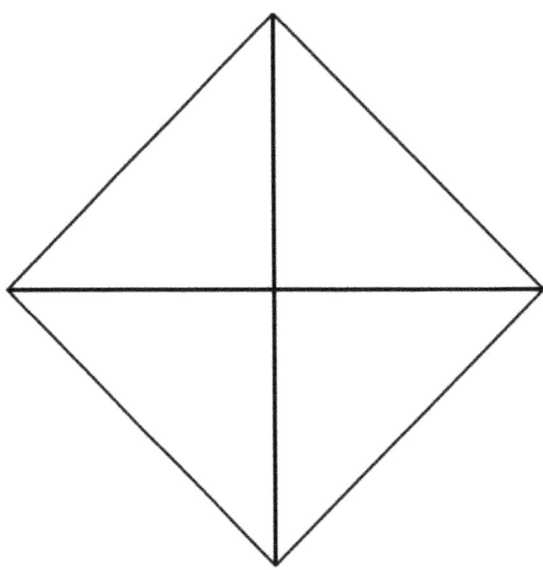

Fig: 14.3.1 A simple 2D output for the shape

The actual code used to create the program

```
import pygame
import math

# Initialize Pygame
pygame.init()

# Screen dimensions
width, height = 800, 600
screen = pygame.display.set_mode((width, height))
pygame.display.set_caption("3D Octahedron")

# Define the vertices of the octahedron
vertices = [0,1]

# Define the edges that connect the vertices
polygons = [[[100, 300,], [300, 300,], [100, 300,]],
        [[100, 300,], [300, 500,], [300, 300,]],
        [[300, 100,], [500, 300,], [500, 300,]],
        [[300, 500,], [300, 300,], [500, 300,]],]

# Main loop
running = True
distance = 5

# Distance for perspective projection
while running:
  for event in pygame.event.get():
  if event.type == pygame.QUIT:
    running = False

  # Clear the screen
  screen.fill((0, 0, 0))

  # Draw the edges
  for i in range(len(polygons)):
```

```
        pygame.draw.line(screen, (0, 255, 255), (polygons[i][0][0],
polygons[i][0][1]),(polygons[i][1][0], polygons[i][1][1]), 1)
        pygame.draw.line(screen, (0, 255, 255), (polygons[i][1][0],
polygons[i][1][1]),(polygons[i][2][1], polygons[i][2][0]), 1)
        pygame.draw.line(screen, (0, 255, 255), (polygons[i][2][0],
polygons[i][2][1]),(polygons[i][0][1], polygons[i][0][0]), 1)

    # Update the display
    pygame.display.flip()

    # Limit frame rate
    pygame.time.Clock().tick(60)

# Quit Pygame
pygame.quit()
```

Summary of chapter

The intention of the chapter was to determine a procedure to simplify drawing a set of polygons onto the screen. The reason for this is that many types of meshes are created using hundreds of polygons at any one time. This often slows down the processor as rendering the object is often overly complicated. By writing the code as a simple loop, the entire process is reduced to a few simple lines of code.

End of Chapter Quiz

Design the dimensions of a simple object.

Define a number of ways meshes are used within 3D programming.

How are individual coordinates separated within a table?

Describe how complex meshes are created.

CHAPTER 15

Rotating octahedron

In this chapter, you will look at the following

- How to design a simple program
- Creatin a complex object
- Applying the polygon unpacker

15.1.1 Designing a complex object out of individual polygons

As we have seen in the previous chapter, a group of polygons can be used to draw the outline of a simple shape. Due to the necessity to produce more complex objects. This chapter explore how to make an octahedron out of a few sets of polygons. This is achieved by using the same set of procedures used to unpack the polygons. Except this program attempts to create the same process for a rotating three-dimensional shape. The program identifies how a set of coordinates might be used to create complicated objects within a 3D environment, and the processes involved to add the dimension and movement to the object.

15.1.2 Flow chart to describe the program

The program used to create the rotating mesh incorporates a loop to alter the position of each of the coordinates in turn. This allows the program to change the position of the polygons as they are drawn onto the screen. The program begins by defining the object as a set of polygons within a list. The vectors used to describe the object are then transformed by the program through a series matrices used to rotate the projected image onto the screen. The program again uses the polygon unpacker to simplify the code used to render the object.

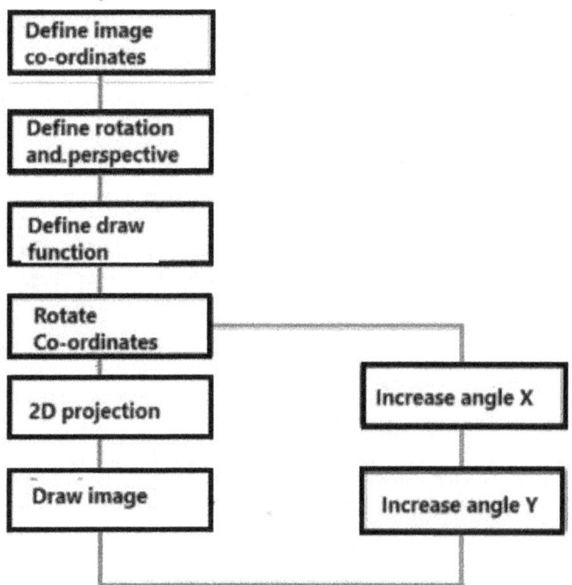

Fig: 15.1.2 Flowchart for the rotating octahedron

15.2.1 Rotation and projection of the object

As with previous examples the movement of the object uses the same form of matrices calculation. Again each vertices used to describe the object are transformed through the calculation, before being drawn onto the screen. The projection for the object is also completed at this stage and allows the image to retain a 3D perspective during each cycle of movement. The code below details how the projection is created during the running of the program.

```
def project(x, y, z, distance):
    factor = distance / (distance + z)
    x_proj = x * factor
    y_proj = y * factor
    return x_proj, y_proj
```

15.2.2 Unpacking the objects shape

The code used to draw the polygons works in a similar way to the program used in the last chapter. The image is redrawn a single polygon at a time. Instead of using a two-coordinate system, a list of edges is used to determine the start and end of each of the polygon's sides. This allows the program to perform the same action of unpacking the polygons. Except the image is now working in 3D and uses a method of drawing each of vertices as a three-coordinate vector.

15.3.1 Running the program

The program used in this chapter will provide the output found below. The image should display a rotating octahedron that moves position. As the image rotates the object should change dimensions so that it is possible to determine the distance from the camera. The object here could be any type of shape, depending on the information used to describe the vertices.

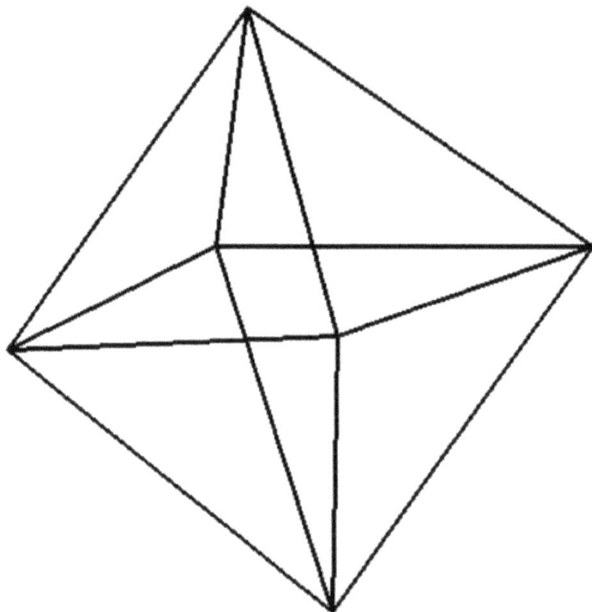

Fig: 15.3.1 Output for the rotating octahedron

```
import pygame
import math

# Initialize Pygame
pygame.init()

# Screen dimensions
width, height = 800, 600
screen = pygame.display.set_mode((width, height))
pygame.display.set_caption("3D Octahedron")

# Define the vertices of the octahedron
vertices = [[1, 0, 0], [-1, 0, 0], [0, 1, 0], [0, -1, 0], [0, 0, 1], [0, 0, -1]]

# Define the edges that connect the vertices
edges = [[0, 2], [0, 3], [0, 4], [0, 5], [1, 2], [1, 3], [1, 4], [1, 5], [2, 4], [2, 5],
[3, 4], [3, 5]]

# Perspective projection
def project(x, y, z, distance):
    factor = distance / (distance + z)
    x_proj = x * factor
    y_proj = y * factor
    return x_proj, y_proj

# Main loop
running = True
angle_x, angle_y, angle_z = 0, 0, 0
distance = 5

# Distance for perspective projection
while running:
    for event in pygame.event.get():
    if event.type == pygame.QUIT:
        running = False

    # Clear the screen
    screen.fill((0, 0, 0))
```

```
    # Rotate the octahedron
    angle_x += 0.01
    angle_y += 0.01
    angle_z += 0.01

    # Transform the vertices
    transformed_vertices = []
    for vertex in vertices:
        x, y, z = vertex
        # Rotate around X axis
        y, z = y * math.cos(angle_x) - z * math.sin(angle_x), y * math.
sin(angle_x) + z * math.cos(angle_x)
        # Rotate around Y axis
        x, z = x * math.cos(angle_y) + z * math.sin(angle_y), -x * math.
sin(angle_y) + z * math.cos(angle_y)
        # Rotate around Z axis
        x, y = x * math.cos(angle_z) - y * math.sin(angle_z), x * math.
sin(angle_z) + y * math.cos(angle_z)
        # Apply perspective projection
        x_proj, y_proj = project(x, y, z, distance)
        # Convert to screen coordinates
        x_screen = int(width / 2 + x_proj * 200)
        y_screen = int(height / 2 - y_proj * 200)
        transformed_vertices.append((x_screen, y_screen))

    # Draw the edges
    for edge in edges:
        pygame.draw.line(screen, (0, 255, 255), transformed_vertices[edge[0]],
transformed_vertices[edge[1]], 1)
    # Update the display
    pygame.display.flip()

# Limit frame rate
pygame.time.Clock().tick(60)

# Quit Pygame
pygame.quit()
```

Summary of chapter

This chapter has explored how to create more complex structures using the polygon unpacker to draw an objects image. This topic is important to the development of 3D programming as many types of software need to use multidimensional objects or models. The shape used within the program had a total of 8 polygons, although the same concept can be use to describe meshes that use thousands of polygons at the same time. The chapter has demonstrated how an object can be built and the type of procedures used to draw the model and project the image onto the screen. The expectation is that this has explained some of the procedures used within 3D programming.

End of Chapter Quiz

Describe how complex objects are created

How does the number of vertices effect processor time?

Draw a shape using only polygons

Write a program to draw a complex mesh.

www.ingramcontent.com/pod-product-compliance
Lightning Source LLC
LaVergne TN
LVHW041205050326
832903LV00020B/471